Chef John Folse's
LOUISIANA SAMPLER

Recipes from Our Fairs & Festivals

by

Chef John D. Folse, CEC, AAC

Chef John Folse
& Company

PUBLISHING

Gonzales, Louisiana

Library of Congress Catalog Card Number: 96–090707

ISBN 0-9625152-3-X

First Printing: October, 1996

If this book is not available at your local bookstore, copies may be ordered directly from:
Chef John Folse & Company
2517 South Phillipe Avenue
Gonzales, LA 70737
(504) 644-6000

Price $19.95 plus $3.50 for shipping and handling (total: $23.45)

Also available:

Chef John Folse's *Evolution of Cajun & Creole Cuisine*
Price: $19.95 plus $3.00 for shipping and handling (total: $22.95)

Chef John Folse's *Plantation Celebrations*
Price: $24.95 plus $3.50 shipping and handling (total: $28.45)

Chef John Folse's *Something Old & Something New*
Price: $22.95 plus $4.50 shipping and handling (total: $27.45)

Designed by Stacey Deen Griffith, assisted by Amanda Lucas, for

1822 Howard Street, Jackson, MS 39302, 601.948.5517

CONTENTS

FOREWORD

Louisiana is by far the best fair, the best festival, I've ever attended. I hope that doesn't sound strange to you, but Louisiana in itself is a food and cultural spectacular! *Louisiana Sampler* could not be a more perfect name for this book! With 7 different cultures — Native American, French, Spanish, English, African, German and Italian — settling this area, all within 100 years of one another and at some point combining their languages, food customs and cultures, a patchwork here in Bayou country was indeed created. In no other state could you hop into an automobile with friends and family and take off, traveling throughout 64 parishes, and sample the melange of culture, landscape and cuisine you will experience here in Louisiana.

As the host of "A Taste of Louisiana," coming to you each week direct from our Louisiana Public Broadcasting studios in Baton Rouge, I've enjoyed the opportunity to visit every village and hamlet on Louisiana's backroads and bayous in discovery of our uniqueness. These travels have given me a tremendous amount of pride in the ability to bring the true taste of Louisiana to you and the thousands of viewers worldwide. In this new book, *Louisiana Sampler*, I hope to share with you a glimpse of not only 26 fairs and festivals, but the towns hosting them and the numerous attractions available to you when visiting these events.

Louisiana's interesting cuisines and cultures have been the topic of millions of newspaper and magazine articles as well as television shows and documentaries for years. It's the uniqueness of Louisiana that brings the media to our state, and nothing creates more excitement than the weekend socials we lovingly call festivals. I can think of no other place on earth where food and friends gathering together is such an integral part of daily life. No matter how small the town, how few members make up the committee, or how varied the food or custom, a festival is likely to pop up overnight. With nearly 400 fairs and festivals already in place, it would be difficult for any other state to catch up with Louisiana when it comes to weekend partying.

What takes place at these festivals in many cases are common to all but often unique to each. Most will have a parade down Main Street, a beauty pageant choosing the festival queen and sometimes a king. Each will feature a cooking contest and just about all will have carnival rides and a shady picnic ground for the family. But, I don't think I've ever seen a caber toss in Cajun country other than at the Celtic Nations Heritage Festival. I've never stirred a caldo pot at any festival other than the Los Islenos Festival in St. Bernard Parish. I've thought about it long and hard, but I've never seen a beautiful girl kiss a frog anywhere but at the Frog Festival in Rayne. I can personally say, I've never slummed with the hogs until I attended the Cochon de Lait Festival in Mansura.

Yes, many of our festivals are one of a kind offering unique activities. I remember escorting the Swine Queen in Basile. I blew a mean duck call in Gueydan. I sprinkled salt over my ice cold watermelon while sitting under a pecan tree in Franklinton. I even carried on a great conversation with the pirate Jean Lafitte at Contraband Days in Lake Charles. Many of you will never know the joy of talking to the 6-year-old boy who won the Yam-I-Mal Contest at the Yambilee Festival in Opelousas, with his creation of Humpty Dumpty using a yam shaped like the fat little fellow which was decorated with broken egg shells. Yes, there's nothing like the experience of a Louisiana fair or festival!

I have absolutely no doubt that debate exists throughout the state as to the origin of most of our festivals. I personally sat in with the organizing committee of the Sunshine Festival in Donaldsonville back in the 1980s when a few guys, including Glenn Falgoust, decided that it was time to honor the Sunshine Bridge, the song "You Are My Sunshine," or the rays of sunshine gleaming off of the Mississippi River in this sleepy little town. It should be pretty obvious to us where and why the Peach, Blueberry, Tomato and Strawberry Festivals get their names and why we pay homage to these delicacies. On the other hand, somebody had to have a sparkle in their eye and a bit of mischief in their spirit when they came together to organize the Makin' Music Festival in Covington, the Buggy Festival in Churchpoint and even the Sulphur Mines Festival in Sulphur. But the reason why should matter not. The fact that people get together joining friends and family over good food, music and crafts is enough for anybody to come and experience a festival.

It's been a great 2 years traveling our state, searching out the fairs and festivals to create our TV series and this *Louisiana Sampler*. I've learned a lot about this place called the Bayou State, its customs and its people, but nothing more important than the simple fact that we're an area filled with color and tradition and we love to celebrate. I've come to know that we're a people who love a good time as much as we love our great food. In all of this, I've come to understand better how we've taken the best from throughout the world and married it in our cast iron pots to create a new culture, a new cuisine and a new land we call Louisiana.

Welcome to Louisiana, and please . . . Sample our fairs and festivals!

THE CHEF

Chef John Folse is the owner and executive chef of his Louisiana based corporations. His Lafitte's Landing Restaurant in Donaldsonville, is recognized as one of the finest restaurants in and around New Orleans. White Oak Plantation, in Baton Rouge, houses his catering and events management company, "Voila!." Louisiana's Premier Products, his cook and chill plant in New Orleans, manufactures soups, sauces, entrees and meats for foodservice and retail establishments across the country. Chef Folse is the author of numerous books and publications available in bookstores nationally.

John is respected around the world as an authority on Cajun and Creole cuisine and culture. He hosts his own national television cooking show on PBS. He has taken his famous "Taste of Louisiana" from Hollywood to the Great Wall of China, opening promotional Louisiana restaurants in Hong Kong, Japan, Beijing, London, Paris, Rome, Bogota, Taipei and Seoul. In 1987, Chef Folse was selected as "Louisiana Restaurateur of the year" by the Louisiana Restaurant Association and in November of 1988, the Louisiana Sales and Marketing Executives named him "Louisiana's Marketing Ambassador to the World." In 1988, Chef Folse made international headlines by opening his "Lafitte's Landing East" in Moscow during the presidential summit between Ronald Reagan and Mikhail Gorbachev. This opening represented the first time an American Restaurant had operated on Soviet soil. Immediately following this venture, John hosted ten Soviet chefs for the first Soviet American Culinary Exchange. In 1989, Chef Folse was invited to create the first ever Vatican State Dinner in Rome, and while there had a private audience with Pope John Paul II. In 1990, Chef Folse was named the "National Chef of the Year" by the American Culinary Federation, the highest honor bestowed upon an American chef. In that same year, his Lafitte's Landing was inducted into the "Fine Dining Hall of Fame," one of ten restaurants in America honored with this prestigious award. In October of 1996, Lafitte's Landing was awarded the DiRoNA (Distinguished Restaurants of North America) Award.

Chef John D. Folse, CEC, AAC

Chef Folse is the recipient of numerous culinary awards and recognitions, and has been honored by local, state and international governments for his continuing efforts to showcase America's regional cooking around the world. His most prestigious acknowledgement to date was Nicholls State University's decision to name their new culinary program in his honor. An Associate of Science in Culinary Arts degree program will begin in January of 1996 with a Bachelor of Science in Culinary Arts degree program beginning in January of 1997. Nicholls State, his Alma Mater, is located in Thibodaux, Louisiana. For additional information on our organization you may locate us on the Internet at: **http:\\www.jfolse.com**

THE PHOTOGRAPHERS

Photographer Jose´ L. Garcia, II collaborated with Chef John Folse in producing each of the color food photographs presented in this book.

Garcia, a native New Orleanian, graduated from Jesuit High School and Tulane University. A professional photographer since 1975, Garcia has operated his own freelance commercial studio based in New Orleans for the past fourteen years. Having pursued assignments ranging from political campaigns to fashion and product catalogs, Garcia began his association with Chef Folse after photographing the family residence where the Chef and his seven siblings were raised. The two soon discovered a common fascination with those things indigenous to Louisiana and the Cajun culture.

Occasionally accompanying Chef Folse to document his domestic travels, Garcia began capturing the chef's culinary art on film in 1982, emphasizing the roots of these Cajun creations by integrating elements of Louisiana culture, tradition or environment into as many of the compositions as possible.

The images are the latest crop to be harvested from this fruitful collaboration.

Bon Appetit!

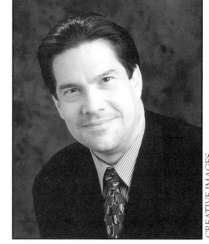

José L. Garcia, II

CREATIVE IMAGES

Bill Castel

KLEINPETER PHOTOGRAPHY

Husband, father, musician and professional photographer — these are but a few of the many hats worn by Bill Castel. As owner of Heritage Photography in Baton Rouge for the past 15 years, Castel is proud of his role as Chef Folse's official photographer for his PBS television series "A Taste of Louisiana."

A graduate of De LaSalle High School in New Orleans, Castel attended Tulane University, majoring in Accounting. He has served in the Air National Guard as a flight instructor repairman and was a musician with the Southern Playboys for 25 years.

The father of three children, Castel is married to the former Carolyn Grisbaum, and they reside in Baton Rouge.

THE DESIGN

A note from the designer, Stacey Deen Griffith

Louisiana Sampler was typeset and designed on a Macintosh, using QuarkXpress and PhotoShop. The title font is Caslon Antique, which has the patina of well-seasoned cast iron and the style of an antique letterpress. The text is set in Goudy. The quilt design elements are high-resolution color scans of my husband Greg's grandmother's antique quilt, with some new fabrics thrown in (i.e.: part of the quilt border in the Black Heritage Festival section is mudcloth from Africa). The line art is from vintage engravings. The fresh herbs were plucked from my garden and a few leaves, herbs and peppers were stolen from the Kantors next door. Thanks go to them and to my mom who mailed me pecans and Spanish moss when I was in a pinch.

THE DESIGNER

For years I have been a fan of Laffite's Landing and Chef John Folse, but it was just a coincidence that a client of mine introduced us, and much to the delight of my family. While I am a Mississippi girl, the roots of my family tree extend into Louisiana. My great-grandfather, Michael Wild, was born in Donaldsonville, where his father was a butcher, though he and most of his ancestors were lumbermen. He moved to New Orleans where he met and married my great-grandmother Juanita Reid, born on Constance Street in the Irish Quarter. My grandmother *Joy Wild* was born New Year's Day in New Orleans. Clearly, festivity runs in the family. My mother Lindy was also born in New Orleans though her parents moved the family to Meridian, Mississippi when she was little, and I, too, grew up there.

My undergraduate studies at the University of Southern Mississippi were in anthropology and archaeology, with a minor in art, and my graduate studies at the University of Mississippi were in anthropology, with an emphasis in cultural anthropology, particularly Southern culture. While dabbling in museum work, I found my calling in design when I acknowledged my affinity for computer graphics and started a business, Grade A Fancy Artworks.

I have developed a niche in the restaurant design field with everything from advertising, menus, t-shirts, product development and packaging to newletters, web sites, woodcut prints, and neon signs in my repertoire. I've designed a wine shop and I art direct *Mississippi Restaurateur* magazine. I also art direct film and video projects, as well as CD ROMs and interactive kiosks. Designing books is probably the most satisfying work I do, especially designing *Louisiana Sampler* with Chef John Folse and his irrepressible assistant, Pamela Castel.

My talented husband Greg is responsible for introducing me to computers and for constantly teaching me new and wonderful things. He is also my favorite critic and I can't thank him enough (especially since I'm working on our fourth anniversary). Greg and I make our home in Jackson, Mississippi.

Stacey Deen Griffith

ROBERT B. DEEN, JR.

CHEF'S EXECUTIVE ASSISTANT

Coordinating the production and printing of this and all other Chef John Folse Cookbooks is his enthusiastic and efficient Executive Assistant Pamela Castel. From concept to printing, Castel plays a vital role in the cookbook production process.

Employed by Chef John Folse & Company since 1988, Castel is a 1981 graduate of Cabrini High School in New Orleans and attended LSU with a major in Special Education. To attempt to list her responsibilities would be impossible. However, when asked to note the projects of which she is most proud, she quickly names the production of Chef John Folse's cookbooks and her role as Coordinating Producer for his internationally-famous PBS series, "A Taste of Louisiana."

In addition to her work in production, Castel is charged with the challenge of scheduling Chef Folse for functions, celebrity appearances, speeches and his international travels promoting Cajun and Creole cuisine worldwide. Whatever the task, Castel is up to the challenge.

You can bet that when you next see Chef John Folse, his right hand, Pamela Castel, is not far behind.

Pamela A. Castel

DEDICATION

If you wish to witness generosity at its best, just ask anyone in Louisiana for help! I cannot think of an instance when we drove into a town, walked into a plantation or pulled up along some lonely backroad and asked for help that the answer wasn't an overwhelming, yes! There are no people in the world who take greater pride or receive more joy in giving than the people of the Bayou State. Without their efforts, this book and its accompanying Louisiana Public Broadcasting Series, "Louisiana's Fairs and Festivals," would not have been possible.

I pay a very special tribute to the over 400 festival chairpersons and committee members, who work diligently throughout the year to create the most spectacular family outings in America, lovingly called festivals. Although I could choose only 26 of your events for this series, I appreciate the enthusiasm and willingness to assist by each and every one of you! I wish to thank the cities and towns, which host these festivals along with the mayors and city councilman who welcomed us as we covered these extravaganzas. You made us feel like true dignitaries, and yes, I do cherish the keys to your city. A special thanks to the hotels and bed-and-breakfasts which honored us with accommodations, including Loyd Hall near Alexandria, leRosier in New Iberia, Maison DaBoval and Maison D'Memoire in Rayne. Thanks for the Southern hospitality and great feather pillows.

What would we be without our sponsors? No book or series would exist without their willingness to commit funding, so our efforts could appear here and on the TV screen. I thank the Louisiana Department of Tourism and Zatarain's, our underwriters. My sincere appreciation to Albertson's Incorporated for the food used in the shooting of our series and the recipe testing. I thank Lodge Cast Iron for supplying us with the fabulous black iron pots. I couldn't cook a thing without them. A special acknowledgement must go to Acadian Ambulance, Air-Med Services for the use of their helicopter in shooting the opening segment of our show and Charley Steen of C.S. Steen's Syrup Mill for funding the ancillary cost associated with that opening. Wow, what a beautiful shot! Thank you Ron Henderson and Ken Fowler for the antique cars that are seen carrying us through the Bayou country each week.

Obviously, there are hundreds of people behind the scenes who come together to make us look great on "A Taste of Louisiana." A special thanks to Louisiana Public Broadcasting: Beth Courtney, President and CEO, Clay Fourrier, Executive Producer, Donna LaFleur, Producer, and Carlos Eaglin, Assistant Producer. I wish to extend my appreciation to the great eyes of our camera operators: Mike Abel, Jodie Fontenot, Rex Fortenberry, Chris Miranda, Keith Normand and Virnardo Woods. To the one person who removes the dark circles from under my eyes and keeps me on time, down to the second, Floor Director, Sally Budd. You wouldn't hear a word I said if it wasn't for my Audio Specialist, Benjamin R. Williams. Last but not least, the person who helps me with the voice-overs and gives me great off-camera instruction, my buddy, Ken Fowler. An extra special thanks to Patti Bollinger Bradley for writing the introduction to each festival and to Sarah Liberta and Dawn Newchurch for searching out the best guest in Louisiana and the background information for the book and series. To my photographers, Bill Castel and Jose Garcia, thanks a million for capturing this entire series on film.

Naturally, as a chef, the most important part of it all is the food! I wish to thank Sharon Jesowshek, my Culinary Coordinator, and Carol Gunter, Warren LaFrance and John Shirley for all of the cooking and styling that makes the food look so spectacular.

To my Administrative Assistant and Coordinating Producer, Pamela Castel, I wish to say a single thanks because there's not enough room in this book to write thank you enough for all that she does for the company, the books or the series.

Finally, to my wife, Laulie, who for the fourth time was drafted to edit the words of this book and gave us proof after proof of finished work, I thank her for her expertise and style.

No festival would take place in Louisiana without the people of this State, who actively participate in all things, food and fun. You, too, welcome us with open arms as we visit your cities and partake of your hospitality. The most heartfelt thanks of all go to you, for after all, it is your culture and cuisine we celebrate!

Chapter One
March

Black Heritage Festival

BLACK HERITAGE FESTIVAL
Lake Charles, Louisiana

To participate in a celebration of the African-American culture like no other, festival-goers will not want to miss the annual Black Heritage Festival. Held in Southwest Louisiana, home to over 75 of Louisiana's festivals, the Black Heritage Festival observes this unique culture through educational, cultural and entertaining activities each year in early March.

For three full days, the Lake Charles Civic Center turns into a celebration where continuous music can be heard resonating throughout the festival. As participants tour historical exhibits, enjoy talent and fashion shows, and gain knowledge about the African-American culture, they will relish in the sounds of Gospel, Jazz, R&B and Zydeco from some of the best known area artists.

Numerous heritage displays feature a wide array of items for sale which represent this culture so important to the history of Louisiana. Educational opportunities abound and blend nicely with the entertainment provided to the guests.

One of the youngest of the Louisiana festivals, the Black Heritage Festival was founded in 1987. Its proceeds support community youth activities, scholarships and classroom teaching aids.

If seeking to know the past will help us to understand the future, this festival provides the perfect vehicle for learning about our cultural past and about a people who sacrificed most to help shape the food, music and culture of Louisiana.

Lagniappe

The City of Lake Charles in Calcasieu Parish is filled with Southwest Louisiana charm featuring vast marshlands, winding rivers and stunning beaches. From Cajun treats to gourmet cuisine, the restaurants cater to all palates. Steamboat Bill's is the place to go for seafood and great Cajun and Creole fare in a relaxed down home atmosphere. One of my favorite restaurants that has been around for over 15 years is Cafe Margaux's. Make sure you tell the waiter that John Folse sent you to eat! Over a dozen bed-and-breakfast and guesthouse accommodations are offered in the city. Both The Claibourne House and the Ramsay-Curtis Mansion, c. 1884 and 1885, feature Queen Anne style architecture and are listed on the National Register of Historic Places.

Travel on I-10 West to Lake Shore Exit and follow directionals to the Lake Charles Civic Center. For more information, call the Lake Charles Convention and Visitors Bureau at (318) 436-9588 or (800) 456-SWLA.

Photo: José L. Garcia, II
Clockwise from bottom left: Blackeyed Pea Congre, Yam Bread, Smothered Seven Steaks

BLACKEYED PEA CONGRE WITH HAM HOCK & SALT MEAT

INGREDIENTS:

1 pound blackeyed peas

$^1/_2$ cup shortening or bacon drippings

1 cup chopped onions

1 cup chopped celery

1 cup chopped red bell pepper

$^1/_4$ cup diced garlic

$^1/_2$ pound salt meat

1 smoked ham hock

1 cup sliced green onions

$^1/_2$ cup chopped parsley

salt and black pepper

Louisiana Gold Pepper Sauce

METHOD:

Rinse beans, removing any hard or discolored beans. The beans will cook faster if they are soaked in cold water overnight in the refrigerator. When ready to cook, rinse beans once again in cold water In a 2-quart sauce pot, melt shortening or bacon drippings over medium-high heat. Add onions, celery, bell pepper and garlic. Saute 3-5 minutes or until vegetables are wilted. Add salt meat and ham hock. Cook 5 additional minutes. Add blackeyed peas and enough cold water to cover beans by approximately 2 inches. Bring mixture to a rolling boil, reduce to simmer and allow to cook 30 minutes, stirring occasionally to keep vegetables from scorching. Continue to cook, stirring occasionally, until peas are tender, approximately 1-1$^1/_2$ hours. Add green onions and parsley. Season to taste using salt, pepper and Louisiana Gold.

PREP TIME: 1$^1/_2$ hours   SERVES: 8

NOTES

_____

_____

_____

_____

_____

_____

YAM BREAD

INGREDIENTS:

2½ cups sugar

1 cup cooking oil

4 eggs

2½ cups sifted flour

2 tsps soda

½ tsp salt

1 tsp cinnamon

1 tsp nutmeg

⅔ cup water

2 cups cooked sweet potatoes, mashed

1 cup chopped pecan

METHOD:

Grease three 9" x 5" loaf pans. Preheat oven to 350 degrees F. In a large mixing bowl, combine sugar and oil and beat well. Add eggs and beat after each addition. In a separate mixing bowl, combine dry ingredients and add egg mixture alternately with water. Stir in sweet potatoes and chopped nuts. Pour batter into 3 pans and bake for 1 hour or until tester comes out clean.

PREP TIME: 1½ hours   MAKES: 3 loaves

LIZZIES

INGREDIENTS:

1 package seedless raisins

½ cup bourbon

¼ cup butter

½ cup light brown sugar

2 eggs

1½ cups all purpose flour

1½ tsps soda

1½ tsp cinnamon

½ tsp nutmeg

½ tsp ground cloves

½ pound pecan halves

½ pound mixed candied fruits

½ pound candied red or green cherries

METHOD:

Preheat oven to 350 degrees F. In a ceramic bowl, place raisins and bourbon. Soak for at least 1 hour to plump. In a mixing bowl, cream butter and gradually beat in sugar. Add eggs, one at a time, beating after each addition. Sift flour, soda and spices into butter mixture. Add raisins, nuts and fruits. Use a teaspoon to drop onto greased cookie sheets. Cut cherries in half and place one on top of each cookie before baking. Bake for 15 minutes or until golden brown.

PREP TIME: 1 hour   SERVES: 3 dozen

NOTES

_____

_____

_____

_____

_____

_____

CATFISH BOULETTES

INGREDIENTS:

6 (8-ounce) catfish fillets
1 pound diced new potatoes
$^{1}/_{4}$ cup diced onions
$^{1}/_{4}$ cup diced celery
2 tbsps diced garlic
$^{1}/_{4}$ cup sliced green onions

2 eggs
$^{1}/_{4}$ cup flour
salt and pepper
Louisiana Gold Pepper Sauce
oil for frying

METHOD:

In a 2-gallon cast iron dutch oven, poach fish. Remove from water and cool. In the same pot, boil potatoes until tender enough to mash. Combine fish, potatoes and all remaining ingredients. Season to taste using salt, pepper and Louisiana Gold. Form mixture into patties, approximately the size of a hamburger. In a 10-inch skillet, heat oil over medium-high heat. Dredge patties in flour and fry until golden brown.

PREP TIME: 1$^{1}/_{2}$ hours   MAKES: 8-10 boulettes

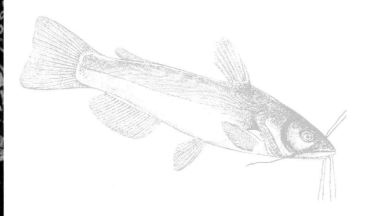

NOTES

_____

_____

_____

_____

_____

_____

SMOTHERED SEVEN STEAKS

INGREDIENTS:

4 pounds seven steaks

4 tbsps cooking oil

1 cup chopped onions

$^1/_2$ cup chopped celery

$^1/_4$ cup chopped red bell pepper

$^1/_4$ cup diced garlic

1 quart beef stock

2 tbsps Worcestershire sauce

$^1/_2$ cup sliced green onions

$^1/_4$ cup chopped parsley

salt and black pepper

Louisiana Gold Pepper Sauce

METHOD:

In a 12-inch cast iron skillet, heat oil over medium-high heat. Add steaks and sear until golden brown. Remove and keep warm. Add onions, celery, bell pepper and garlic. Saute 3-5 minutes or until vegetables are wilted. Return steaks to skillet and add stock and Worcestershire. Bring mixture to a rolling boil, reduce to simmer, cover and cook for approximately $2^1/_2$ hours. Add green onions and parsley and season to taste using salt, pepper and Louisiana Gold. This dish is also excellent baked. Bake for 2 -$2^1/_2$ hours at 375 degrees F. Serve over rice or mashed potatoes.

PREP TIME: $3^1/_2$ hours   SERVES: 6

NOTES

_____

_____

_____

_____

_____

_____

Chapter Two
April

Festival International de Louisiane
Strawberry Festival

FESTIVAL INTERNATIONAL DE LOUISIANE
Lafayette, Louisiana

For six days each April the multi-cultural influences of the Southwest Louisiana city of Lafayette grow by grand proportions. For it is during these six days that this city transforms itself into an unforgettable celebration combining the best in international arts, music, cinema and cuisine. With over 600 performers, enough to rival even this state's largest festivals, its mere scale creates worldwide appeal.

The multitude of food vendors at the festival will make your mouth water with local and international flavors - mouth-watering seafood, spicy hot jambalaya, delicate pastas and Creole gumbo.

The essence of Festival International is a celebration of the arts. You can find music ranging from a Calypso beat to a Cajun waltz. You can discover visual and performing artists in galleries and theaters throughout Lafayette. Theater, dance, cinema and visual arts are all magnificently represented at this festival.

Children will be spellbound by the games, storytellers, music and variety of special programs and activities designed especially for them, many which teach the children about the culture.

The Festival International de Louisiane seeks to enrich the community by celebrating its native cultures and to educate the public as to the historical achievements and artistic expressions of related global cultures. It accomplishes these goals and much more. This is a grand celebration of a culture, of a people, that you will surely not want to miss.

Lagniappe

While in Lafayette for the festival, you may want to explore top attractions that will give you an in-depth look into this area's cultural past. Some of the best are the Acadian Cultural Center Jean Lafitte National Park, the Acadian Village and Vermilionville.

Bed-and-breakfast lodging is abundant in the area. La Grande Maison in nearby Broussard is a popular choice. If you want to kick up your feet to great Cajun music, visit Randal's Restaurant and Cajun Dancehall, Enola Prudhomme's, Prejean's and Mulate's in Breaux Bridge.

For a glimpse into life in some of the small, neighboring Cajun towns, take a drive through nearby Carencro, Broussard, Breaux Bridge and New Iberia, home of Bruce Foods Corporation, makers of Louisiana Gold Pepper Sauce and other fine Louisiana Products. Travel to Lafayette via I-49 from the North, I-10 from the East or West, or Highway 90 from the South. The festival is free. For more information, call the Lafayette Convention & Visitors Commission at (800) 346-1958, (800) 543-5340 (Canada) or (318) 232-3737.

Photo: José L. Garcia, II
Chicken and Maque Choux Casserole

SMOTHERED CHICKEN AND MAQUE CHOUX CASSEROLE

INGREDIENTS:

1 (3-pound) fryer chicken, cut into serving pieces

$^1/_2$ cup bacon drippings

4 ears fresh corn

1 cup shopeg corn

1 cup whole kernel corn

2 cups (150-200 count) shrimp, peeled and deveined

1 cup chopped onions

$^1/_2$ cup chopped celery

$^1/_2$ cup chopped green bell pepper

$^1/_2$ cup chopped red bell pepper

$^1/_4$ cup diced garlic

$^1/_4$ cup finely diced andouille

2 cups coarsely chopped tomatoes

2 tbsps tomato sauce

1 quart chicken stock

1 cup sliced green onions

salt and black pepper

Louisiana Gold Pepper Sauce

METHOD:

Preheat oven to 375 degrees F. Select tender, well-developed ears of corn and remove shucks and silk. Using a sharp knife, cut length-wise through the kernels to remove them from the cob. Scrape each cob using the blade of the knife to remove all milk and additional pulp from the corn. This is important since the richness of the dish will depend on how much milk and pulp can be scraped from the cobs. In a 7-quart cast iron dutch oven, melt bacon drippings over medium-high heat. Saute chicken in oil until golden brown on each side. Add corn, onions, celery, bell peppers, garlic and andouille. Saute 3-5 minutes or until vegetables are wilted. Add tomatoes, tomato sauce, stock and shrimp. Continue cooking until juices from the tomatoes and shrimp are rendered into the dish, approximately 15-20 minutes. Add green onions and season to taste using salt and pepper. Cover dutch oven and bake 1 hour until chicken is tender and the full flavors of corn and shrimp are developed.

PREP TIME: 1$^1/_2$ hours   SERVES: 6

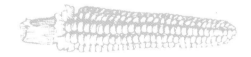

NOTES

_____

_____

_____

_____

_____

RABBIT AND OYSTER MUSHROOM SAUCE PIQUANTE

INGREDIENTS:

3 pounds rabbit
1 cup sliced oyster mushrooms
³/₄ cup oil
³/₄ cup flour
1 cup chopped onions
1 cup chopped celery
¹/₂ cup red bell pepper
¹/₄ cup diced garlic
1 (8-ounce) can tomato sauce
1 cup diced tomatoes

2 whole bay leaves
¹/₂ tsp fresh thyme
¹/₂ tsp fresh basil
¹/₄ cup chopped jalapenos
3 quarts beef stock
1 cup sliced green onions
1 cup chopped parsley
salt and cayenne pepper
Louisiana Gold Pepper Sauce

METHOD:

Cut rabbit into 8 serving pieces. In a 2-gallon cast iron sauce pot, heat oil over medium-high heat. Add flour and, using a wire whisk, stir constantly until dark brown roux is achieved. Add rabbit and cook 10-15 minutes. Add onions, celery, bell pepper, garlic and mushrooms. Saute until vegetables are wilted, approximately 3-5 minutes. Add tomato sauce and diced tomatoes, blending well into roux mixture. Add bay leaves, thyme, basil and jalapenos. Slowly add stock, stirring constantly until all is incorporated. Bring to a low boil, reduce to simmer and cook 45 minutes. Add additional stock if necessary to retain volume. Add green onions and parsley and cook 15 additional minutes. Season to taste using salt, pepper and Louisiana Gold. Adjust seasonings if necessary. Serve over hot white rice or pasta.

PREP TIME: 1 hour   SERVES: 6

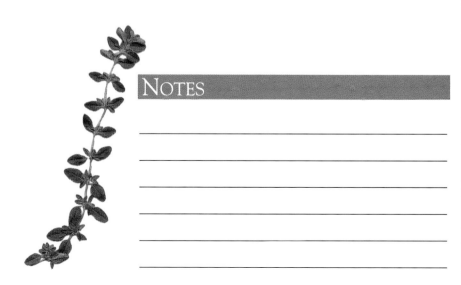

NOTES

_____
_____
_____
_____
_____
_____

STUFFED HARDSHELL CRAB

INGREDIENTS:

2 pounds white or claw crabmeat

6 crab shells, cleaned

$^3/_4$ cup melted butter

2 cups chopped onions

1 cup chopped celery

1 cup chopped bell pepper

1 cup chopped red bell pepper

$^1/_4$ cup diced garlic

1 egg

$^1/_4$ cup heavy whipping cream

salt and black pepper

Louisiana Gold Pepper Sauce

2 cups seasoned Italian bread crumbs

METHOD:

Have your seafood supplier clean and package twelve hardshell crabs. These shells will freeze well, so you may consider buying them well in advance. In a 10-inch cast iron skillet, heat butter over medium -high heat. Add onions, celery, bell peppers and garlic. Saute 3-5 minutes or until vegetables are wilted. Add egg, whipping cream and crabmeat, blending well into vegetable mixture. Cook until all ingredients are tender. Season to taste using salt and pepper. Remove from heat and sprinkle in bread crumbs, a little at a time, until proper consistency is achieved. Stuffing should not be too dry. Adjust seasonings if necessary. Place equal amounts of stuffing in each crab shell and continue until stuffing is used. Additional bread crumbs may be sprinkled on top of stuffed crab. Allow to cool and wrap individually for the freezer or drizzle with a small amount of melted butter and bake at 350 degrees F for approximately 15-20 minutes.

PREP TIME: 1 hours   SERVES: 6

NOTES

_____

_____

_____

_____

_____

STUFFED MUSHROOMS DOMINIQUE YOUX

INGREDIENTS:

24 jumbo fresh mushrooms
$^1/_4$ pound butter
$1^1/_2$ cups chopped mushroom stems
$^1/_2$ cup finely diced green onions
$^1/_4$ cup finely chopped parsley
1 tbsp finely diced garlic
$^1/_4$ cup diced tasso
$^1/_4$ cup diced red bell pepper
1 pound crawfish tails

1 ounce sherry
1 tsp lemon juice
salt and black pepper
Louisiana Gold Pepper Sauce
$^1/_2$ cup seasoned Italian bread crumbs
$^1/_4$ pound melted butter
4 ounces sherry
2 ounces dry white wine

METHOD:

Preheat oven to 450 degrees F. Wash mushrooms well, remove stems and finely chop stems for recipe. In a 10-inch cast iron skillet, melt butter over medium-high heat. Add mushroom stems, green onions, parsley, garlic, tasso and red bell pepper. Saute until vegetables are wilted, approximately 3-5 minutes. Add crawfish, 1 ounce of sherry and lemon juice. Continue cooking an additional 2-3 minutes. Season mixture to taste using salt, pepper and Louisiana Gold. Add bread crumbs, a little at a time, until stuffing is of proper texture, not too dry. Using a teaspoon, fill each mushroom cap with a generous serving of stuffing. Place four mushrooms in each of six au gratin dishes and drizzle with additional melted butter, sherry and white wine. Bake for 10-15 minutes or until mushrooms are golden brown.

PREP TIME: 45 minutes   SERVES: 6

NOTES

_____

_____

_____

_____

_____

_____

25

PETIT POIS WITH TASSO

INGREDIENTS:

2 (17-ounce) cans English peas, drained
1/2 cup butter
1/4 cup flour
1/2 cup diced tasso*
1 cup chopped onions

1/2 cup chopped celery
1/4 cup diced red bell pepper
1 cup sliced mushrooms
salt and black pepper
Louisiana Gold Pepper Sauce

*Tasso is a dried smoked Cajun ham that is seasoned with cayenne pepper, garlic and salt then smoked over pecan wood. The word tasso is believed to have come from the Spanish word "tasajo" which is dried, cured meat. Although this delicacy is often thinly sliced and eaten alone, it is primarily used as a pungent seasoning for vegetables, gumbos and soups.

METHOD:

In a 3-quart cast iron dutch oven, melt butter over medium high heat. Sprinkle in flour and, using a wire whisk, stir constantly until light brown roux is achieved. Add tasso, onions, celery, bell pepper and mushrooms. Saute 3-5 minutes or until vegetables are wilted. Add peas and stir fry an additional 10 minutes. Season to taste using salt, pepper and Louisiana Gold.

PREP TIME: 30 minutes   SERVES: 6

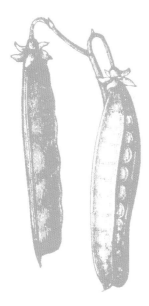

NOTES

_____

_____

_____

_____

_____

STRAWBERRY FESTIVAL
Ponchatoula, Louisiana

If you have ever eaten sweet, red Louisiana strawberries, it is likely that they were grown in the "Strawberry Capital of the World," Ponchatoula, Louisiana. For two days each April since 1972, this city has celebrated one of Louisiana's most important agricultural industries by hosting the Ponchatoula Strawberry Festival. Organizers say April is the most fitting month for the festival since it is the month "when nature bestows upon us her most nearly perfect weather for the strawberries."

Established in 1820, Ponchatoula proves to be an ideal setting for the festival. Originally a logging camp, the only road which once led into the town was part of the Old Spanish Trail. Today, the area is the largest Strawberry producer in the state where farming and timber are still a large part of the local economy.

Drawing almost a quarter of a million people annually, the Strawberry Festival has become one of the most well-attended gatherings in the state. Of course, who can resist streets lined with the delicious, red delicacy prepared in countless ways — Strawberry Shortcake, Strawberry Bread, Strawberry Jam, Chocolate-Dipped Strawberries, and just plain red ripe strawberries plucked right from the plant. The hard task is selecting the best flat of the ripe berries to take home with you since they are all so gorgeous. Don't forget to top off your tasty treats of the day with a cold Strawberry Daiquiri.

While at the festival, take in the sights and sounds of Ponchatoula. With a parade featuring the Strawberry Festival Queen, over 50 festival booths, carnival rides, musical groups, and special events like the Strawberry Eating Contest, you'll have no trouble having a "berry" good time.

Lagniappe

In addition to its reputation as the "Strawberry Capital of the World," Ponchatoula is also America's Antique City. The old town area was recently developed into an antique center with numerous antique dealers offering the finest of "yesterday." This historic downtown area features over 100 art, craft and antique shops and galleries. While in the area, get a cozy night's rest at the Belle Rose Mansion or the Grand Magnolia bed-and-breakfast. Be sure to dine at C'est Bon Restaurant or sample the finest Bavarian pastries in the South at A Taste of Bavaria Bakery.

Neighboring cities to the east, Covington and Mandeville, offer family entertainment and dining options, while New Orleans is only a one-hour drive to the south across Lake Ponchartrain. Travel to Ponchatoula just south of the I-55 and I-12 intersection. For more information, call the local tourist commission at (504) 542-7520 or the Ponchatoula Chamber of Commerce at (504) 386-2533.

Photo: Jose´ L. Garcia, II
Clockwise from bottom left: Lafitte's Pepper-Seared Lamb Chops, Strawberry Daiquiri

STRAWBERRY BREAD

INGREDIENTS:

1 cup strawberry preserves

1/2 cup chopped pecans

1 cup butter

1 1/2 cups sugar

1 tsp vanilla

1 tsp salt

1 tsp lemon juice or lemon extract

4 eggs

1/2 cup sour cream

3 cups flour

1 tsp red food coloring

METHOD:

Preheat oven to 350 degrees F. In a large mixing bowl, place butter, sugar, vanilla, salt and lemon juice or extract. Blend well until all ingredients are well incorporated. Beat in eggs, one at a time. Add sour cream to the egg mixture. Fold in flour, nuts, preserves and food coloring. Pour batter into 2 greased 9" x 5" loaf pans. Bake for 40 minutes or until the bread pulls away from the pan.

PREP TIME: 1 hour   SERVES: 8

STRAWBERRY BALLS

INGREDIENTS:

1/2 cup strawberry wine

1 1/2 cups ground pecans

3 cups ground vanilla wafers

3 tbsps cocoa

3 tbsps white corn syrup

1 tsp vanilla

1 cup powdered sugar

METHOD:

In a large mixing bowl, combine all of the above ingredients. Roll into 1- or 1 1/2-inch balls and roll in powdered sugar.

PREP TIME: 30 minutes   SERVES: 10

NOTES

_____

_____

_____

_____

_____

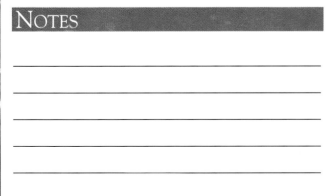

STRAWBERRY DAIQUIRI

INGREDIENTS:

2 pints fresh strawberries or
   1 (12-ounce) package frozen strawberries
10 cups crushed ice
1 cup light rum

2 tbsps lime juice
2 tbsps sugar
$^1/_4$ cup strawberry liqueur

METHOD:

In the bowl of an electric blender, place strawberries, ice, rum, lime juice, sugar and liqueur. Blend for 10-15-second intervals until all ingredients are thoroughly blended. Pour frappe into chilled cocktail or champagne glasses. Before serving, garnish with fresh strawberries and mint.

PREP TIME: 30 minutes   MAKES: 6 drinks

VERY STRAWBERRY BUTTER

INGREDIENTS:

$^1/_4$ pound unsalted butter
$2^1/_2$ tbsps strawberry preserves
$^1/_4$ cup chopped strawberries

METHOD:

In a small mixing bowl, beat butter with a wooden spoon until creamy, almost the texture of sour cream. Beat in preserves, 1 tablespoon at a time. The butter will acquire a curdled look, but do not worry. Mix in chopped strawberries. Place butter in a serving bowl and refrigerate for a couple of hours. Prior to serving, allow butter to reach room temperature before stirring.

PREP TIME: 20 minutes   MAKES: $^1/_2$ cup

NOTES

_____

_____

_____

_____

_____

_____

LAFITTE'S PEPPER SEARED LAMB CHOPS

INGREDIENTS:

12 lamb chops, 1/2-inch thick
1/4 cup ground pink peppercorns
1/4 cup ground black peppercorns
1 cup seasoned flour
1/2 cup oil
1/2 cup sliced green onions
1 tbsp diced garlic

1 cup oyster mushrooms
1 tsp chopped thyme
1 ounce strawberry wine
1 tbsp strawberry jam
1/4 cup sliced strawberries
2 cups demi-glace or beef gravy
salt and cracked pepper

METHOD:

Place the lamb chops on a large platter and evenly coat both sides with crushed pepper-corns. Set aside. In a 10-inch cast iron skillet, heat oil over medium-high heat. Dust chops in flour, shaking off all excess. Saute until golden brown on both sides or medium rare. Remove chops, set aside and keep warm. Into the skillet, add onions, garlic, mushrooms and thyme. Saute 3-5 minutes or until vegetables are wilted. Remove the pan from the burner and add strawberry wine. NOTE: Be careful as alcohol will ignite and burn a few minutes until the flame extinguishes itself. Add strawberry jam, strawberries and demi-glace. Season to taste using salt and pepper. Swirl the skillet above the burner until the jam and demi-glace are well incorporated. Bring to a rolling boil, reduce sauce until slightly thickened and return chops to pan. Heat 2-3 minutes and serve with sauce.

PREP TIME: 45 minutes   SERVES: 6

NOTES

_____

_____

_____

_____

_____

_____

DROP BISCUITS PONCHATOULA

INGREDIENTS:

1³/₄ cups all purpose flour

3 tsps baking powder

¹/₂ tsp salt

6 tbsps softened butter

1 cup buttermilk

METHOD:

Preheat oven to 450 degrees F. In a large mixing bowl, combine flour, baking powder and salt. Mix thoroughly and, using a fork, blend in butter until dough is formed. Make a well in the center of the dough mixture and pour in buttermilk. Stir the dough 1-2 minutes or until buttermilk is well blended into the mixture. Using a large mixing spoon, drop twelve equal amounts of the mixture onto an ungreased baking sheet. This procedure will create inconsistent shapes which will look more homemade then a cut biscuit. Bake for 15 minutes on the center oven rack or until the biscuits are evenly browned. Remove from oven and brush with melted butter before serving. Here in Bayou country, we mix ¹/₂ cup softened butter with 1 tablespoon of Steen's cane syrup for a great topping for hot drop biscuits.

PREP TIME: 30 minutes   MAKES: 12 biscuits

SCONES

INGREDIENTS:

2 cups all purpose flour

1 tbsp baking powder

¹/₂ tsp salt

6 tbsp butter

¹/₂ cup milk

1 egg

2 tbsp honey

¹/₂ cup currants

METHOD:

Preheat oven to 425 degrees F. In a large mixing bowl, combine flour, baking powder and salt. Cut butter into dry ingredients until the mixture resembles coarse cornmeal. Combine milk, egg and honey. Stir into dry ingredients until moistened. Knead 15 times on a floured surface. Divide dough in half and form into 2 balls. Roll or pat each one ¹/₂-inch thick, forming 2 six-inch circles. Cut each circle into 6 wedges. Bake on a ungreased baking sheet for 12 minutes or until golden brown.

PREP TIME: 30 minutes   MAKES: 12

NOTES

_____

_____

_____

_____

_____

_____

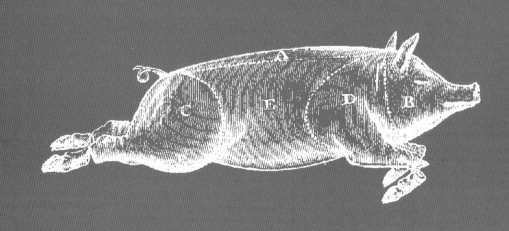

Chapter Three
May

Breaux Bridge Crawfish Festival
Cochon de Lait Festival

Breaux Bridge Crawfish Festival
Breaux Bridge, Louisiana

If you have been to Mardi Gras in New Orleans, you have experienced the largest tourism event in the state. To experience the second largest annual event in Louisiana, you have to travel to the small town of Breaux Bridge during the first full weekend in May. The Breaux Bridge Crawfish Festival, which draws hundreds of thousands of tourists and locals each year, celebrates that symbol most associated with the Cajun people and South Louisiana — the swamp crawfish.

The little Cajun village on the banks of Bayou Teche brought national attention to Louisiana and its crawfish when it celebrated its centennial in 1959 with much fanfare. It was this year that the Louisiana Legislature named the town of 5,000 "La Capitole Mondiale des Ecrevisseres," the "Crawfish Capital of the World." When the annual festival caught the attention of national newspapers such as *The New York Times*, people increasingly became interested in traveling to Louisiana to be a part of the excitement, eat the exotic food, and absorb a little Cajun culture.

The festival features tons of the crustacean boiled to perfection. The recipes usually include salt, pepper, garlic, onions, lemons and a commercial crawfish boil seasoning for the spicy brew. After boiling for 10 to 12 minutes and allowed to soak for another 15 minutes, the crawfish are ready to serve by the pound. Of course, the festival revelers can also enjoy the famous namesake prepared in every way imaginable — Fried Crawfish, Crawfish Etouffee, Crawfish Dogs, Crawfish Jambalaya, Crawfish Boudin, Crawfish Pies, Crawfish Bisque, and even stuffed in a Cajun Pistol, a specialty sandwich.

Atop several stages, world-famous Cajun and Zydeco musicians gather to entertain the multitudes. Young and old alike join in on the dance floors. The Cajun Music Workshops held in the Heritage Tent are also a big draw. Music takes to the streets, and the town takes on a Mardi Gras-like atmosphere, during the parade.

Participants would not enjoy the festival to its fullest without joining in on the Crawfish Eating Contest (winners are known to eat over 30 lbs. in one sitting), the Crawfish Etouffee Contest, the Cajun Dance Contest or the very popular Crawfish Races, after which the victorious crustacean is mounted and preserved. Artisans and craftsmen from throughout the area also display unique wares for show and sale. And while on the grounds, look for the Crawfish Queen and her King. Little Miss and Master Pincher may also be on hand.

Don't miss this opportunity to travel to the heart of Cajun Country and experience THE festival of Louisiana, the Breaux Bridge Crawfish Festival, a crustacean celebration like no other.

Lagniappe

While in town, try out Cynthia and Dickie Breaux's Duck and Andouille Gumbo at Cafe Des Amis on East Bridge Street. You also can't go wrong getting a bite to eat at Poche's Market and Restaurant on Main Highway or nearby Mulate's Cajun Restaurant along Highway 94. For a place to lay your head down, Country Oaks Guest House, an 1830s Acadian farmhouse, is a good choice. Half Pint's Swamp Adventures, departing from McGee's Landing in Breaux Bridge, is a great way to explore the beauty and serenity of the Atchafalaya Basin. The Acadian city of Lafayette is only minutes to the west of Breaux Bridge. There you can visit Vermilionville, a living history museum, and the Acadian Village, a 19th century village depicting the Acadian lifestyle. Louisiana's capital city of Baton Rouge is a mere 45 minutes to the east. Take Breaux Bridge Exit 109 off I-10 and travel south on Rees Street to the Parc Hardy Festival Grounds. Admissions is $5 per day; free for 13 years and under. An advance three-day pass is $10. For more information, call the Breaux Bridge Crawfish Festival Association, Inc. at (318) 332-6655.

Photo: Jose´ L. Garcia, II
Clockwise from bottom left: Carol Gunter, David Buchanan, Darren Wakefield

FRIED SOFTSHELL CRAWFISH

INGREDIENTS FOR BATTER:

1 cup milk
3 tbsps Creole mustard
$\frac{1}{2}$ cup water

salt and cracked black pepper
1 egg

METHOD:

In a 1-quart mixing bowl, combine all of the above ingredients. Whisk with a wire whip to ensure mixture is well blended. Set aside.

INGREDIENTS FOR BREADING:

2 cups Zatarain's fish fry
$1\frac{1}{2}$ tsps cracked black pepper
$2\frac{1}{4}$ tsps salt

$1\frac{1}{2}$ tsps cayenne pepper
$1\frac{1}{2}$ tsps granulated garlic
$1\frac{1}{2}$ tsps dry thyme

METHOD:

In a 1-quart mixing bowl, combine all of the above ingredients. Whisk with a wire whip to ensure mixture is well blended. Set aside.

INGREDIENTS FOR FRYING:

1 pound softshell crawfish
$1\frac{1}{2}$ quarts vegetable oil

METHOD:

In a home-style deep fryer, such as a Fry Daddy or Fry Baby, preheat oil according to manufacturer's directions, or to 375 degrees F. Place softshell crawfish in batter mixture and allow to set 10-15 minutes. Drain all excess liquid from crawfish and bread well in fish fry. Shake off all excess breading and deep fry a few at a time until crawfish turn golden brown and float to top of frying unit. Remove and drain on paper towels and serve hot, with cocktail or tartar sauce.

PREP TIME: 30 minutes   SERVES: 6

NOTES

_____

_____

_____

_____

LOUISIANA CRAWFISH ETOUFFEE

INGREDIENTS:

2 pounds cleaned crawfish tails
1/4 pound butter
1 cup chopped onions
1 cup chopped celery
1/2 cup chopped green bell pepper
1/2 cup chopped red bell pepper
1/2 cup diced tomatoes
2 tbsps diced garlic
2 bay leaves

1/2 cup tomato sauce
1 cup flour
2 quarts crawfish stock or water
1 ounce sherry
1 cup chopped green onions
1/2 cup chopped parsley
salt and black pepper
Louisiana Gold Pepper Sauce

METHOD:

In a 5 quart cast iron dutch oven, melt butter over medium-high heat. Add onions, celery, bell peppers, tomatoes, garlic and bay leaves. Saute 3-5 minutes or until vegetables are wilted. Add half of the craw-fish tails and tomato sauce, blending well into the mixture. Using a cooking spoon, blend flour into the vegetable mixture to form a white roux. Slowly add crawfish stock or water, a little at a time, until all is incorporated. Bring to a low boil, reduce to simmer and cook 30 minutes, stirring occasionally. Add remaining crawfish tails, sherry, green onions and parsley. Cook an additional 5 minutes. Season to taste using salt and pepper. Serve over steamed white rice or pasta, spicing with a few dashes of Louisiana Gold.

PREP TIME: 1 hour   SERVES: 6

NOTES

_____

_____

_____

_____

_____

_____

CRAWFISH & ANDOUILLE ON ANGEL HAIR PASTA

INGREDIENTS:

1/2 cup cooked crawfish tails
1/4 pound butter
1 tbsp chopped garlic
1/4 cup diced red bell pepper
1/4 cup sliced mushrooms
1/2 cup diced tomatoes
1/2 cup diced andouille
1 ounce dry white wine

1 tbsp lemon juice
2 cups heavy whipping cream
1/4 cup sliced green onions
1/4 pound chipped cold butter
1 tbsp chopped parsley
 salt and black pepper
4 cups cooked angel hair pasta

METHOD:

In a 3-quart cast iron sauce pan, melt butter over medium-high heat. Add garlic, bell pepper, mushrooms, tomatoes and andouille. Saute 3-5 minutes or until all vegetables are wilted. Add crawfish and cook for an additional 2 minutes. Deglaze pan with white wine and lemon juice, and continue cooking until volume of liquid is reduced to one half. Add heavy whipping cream and, stirring constantly, reduce until cream is thick and of a sauce-like consistency, approximately 10 minutes. Add green onions and chipped butter, 2-3 pats at a time, swirling pan constantly over burner. Do not stir with a spoon, as butter will break down and separate if hot spots develop in the pan. Continue adding butter until all is incorporated. Remove from heat, add parsley, and season to taste using salt and pepper. Gently fold in cooked pasta and serve. May be chilled and served as a cold pasta salad.

PREP TIME: 45 minutes   SERVES: 6-8

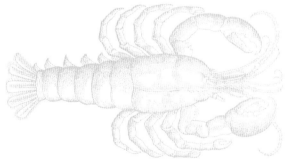

NOTES

_____

_____

_____

_____

_____

_____

BOILED CRAWFISH

INGREDIENTS:

50 pounds cleaned crawfish

30 quarts cold water

12 medium onions, quartered

6 heads of garlic, split in half, exposing pods

4 whole artichokes

2 pounds smoked sausage, sliced

1 dozen lemons, quartered

1 quart vegetable oil

4 pounds salt

$\frac{1}{4}$ pound cayenne pepper

4 (3-ounce) bags Zatarain's crab boil

3 (12-ounce) bottles of beer

24 medium red potatoes

12 ears of corn

METHOD:

Live crawfish may be purchased already washed from your seafood supplier. However, a second rinsing in cold water would not hurt. The purging of crawfish, that is, washing the crawfish in cold salted water, has been found to be useless other than to place the animal under unnecessary stress. So forget the purging — rinsing in cold water will suffice. In a 60-quart stockpot, bring water to a rolling boil. Add onions, garlic, artichokes, sausage, lemons, cooking oil, salt, pepper, crab boil and beer. Allow mixture to continue boiling for 30 minutes. This boiling of the vegetables will ensure a good flavor in the boiling liquid. Add red potatoes and cook approximately 10-12 minutes. Add corn and cook 10 minutes before adding the crawfish. Once the water returns to a boil, cook crawfish 5 minutes, turn off heat and allow the crawfish to sit in boiling liquid 10 additional minutes. Crawfish should be served hot with potatoes, corn and pitchers of ice cold beer.

PREP TIME: 2 hours   SERVES: 12

NOTES

_____

_____

_____

_____

_____

_____

FRIED POPCORN CRAWFISH

INGREDIENTS:

1 pound cleaned crawfish tails

1 quart oil for deep frying

1 egg

1 cup milk

1 cup water

1 cup Zatarain's fish fry

1 tsp fresh thyme, chopped

1 tsp fresh basil, chopped

salt and black pepper

Louisiana Gold Pepper Sauce

METHOD:

In a home-style deep fryer such as a Fry Daddy or Fry Baby, preheat oil according to manufacturer's directions or to 350 degrees F. Season crawfish using thyme, basil, salt, pepper and Louisiana Gold. Prepare an eggwash by combining egg, milk and water. Season eggwash to taste using salt and pepper. Dip crawfish in eggwash then in fish fry. Deep fry until golden brown. Serve with a dipping sauce or on lettuce as a salad.

PREP TIME: 30 minutes   SERVES: 4

NOTES

_____

_____

_____

_____

_____

_____

COCHON DE LAIT FESTIVAL
Mansura, Louisiana

Right in the geographic center of Louisiana, not far from the Mississippi border, lies a town known for its French traditions — and one tradition in particular. Mansura is its name and the Cochon de Lait its claim to fame.

It was in 1960 when Mansura, the sleepy town nestled on scenic Louisiana Highway 1 in Avoyelles Parish, celebrated its 100th year of incorporation with a Cochon de Lait in true French style. The festive atmosphere, combined with the excitement of renewing a long unpracticed style of cooking pig, prompted city officials to begin the annual festival and give the town the exclusive title of "La Capitale de Cochon de Lait," or "The Cochon de Lait Capital."

The town is said to have been named by ex-soldiers of Napoleon, early settlers, who had been with him on his Egyptian campaigns and who saw a resemblance between the Avoyelles prairie lands and Mansura Egypt. Now, thousands flock to the town during Mother's Day weekend each May to catch a glimpse, and a taste, of the pigs, 20 to 30 pounds, lined up in rows over a very hot, open, hickory fire. They are turned constantly for six to eight hours until they are golden brown. The slow cooking produces a wonderful aroma, and the wait is well worth it since this early tradition of cooking pig produces a flavor not quickly forgotten.

Although the festival was discontinued during the late 70s and early 80s, after the townspeople needed a rest from several years of much success, it was resurrected in 1987 and now once again draws large crowds of people from across the state and bordering Mississippi to enjoy the feast and festivities.

So, as the townspeople of Mansura like to say, "Follow your noses to the smell of Cochon de Lait cooking over hot coals." You will end up at one of the best, spring festivals our great state has to offer.

Lagniappe

While visiting in Mansura, consider catching a meal at Kyrle's Restaurant and staying at the nearby Victorian House Bed and Breakfast. Attractions in the area include the DeFosse House if you are an antiques enthusiast and the Tunica Indian Reservations. For a short excursion out of town, visitors are only 35 miles from Alexandria, Bunkie and Chenyville, home of Loyd Hall Plantation and Lea's Pies, 75 miles from Lafayette and 80 miles from the capital city of Baton Rouge.

Take I-49 to Highway 1. Follow Highway 1 to the festival grounds at the Mansura Pavilion. For more information, contact the Mansura Chamber of Commerce at P.O. Box 536, Mansura, Louisiana 71350 or call (318) 964-2887.

Photo: Jose´ L. Garcia, II
Clockwise from bottom left: Hog's Head Cheese, Boudin, Pork Stew and Turnips, Cochon de Lait Pig

HOG'S HEAD CHEESE
(without the head)

INGREDIENTS:

6 pounds pork shoulder

6 pig's feet

10 cups water

2 onions, quartered

3 cups sliced green onions

2 bay leaves

1$^1/_2$ tsps cayenne pepper

1$^1/_2$ tsps salt

$^1/_2$ tsp black pepper

3 pkgs unflavored gelatin

1 cup chopped parsley

1 cup minced carrots

1 cup finely diced red bell pepper

METHOD:

Prepare gelatin according to package directions using 2 cups of the water. Set aside. Cut pork shoulder into 1-inch cubes and place in a large stock pot along with pig's feet and water. Add onions, 1$^1/_2$ cups green onions, bay leaves, cayenne, salt and pepper. Bring to a rolling boil, reduce to simmer and cook until meat falls from the bone, approximately 2 hours. Remove the meat from the liquid and strain solids from the stock. Reserve the liquid and discard vegetables. Once the meat is cooled, debone and grind or chop it finely. Return liquid to the stock pot and bring to a rolling boil. Add gelatin, ground meat, remaining green onions, parsley and vegetables. Cook 10 minutes, remove from heat and allow to cool slightly. Ladle the mixture into two or three 4" x 8" loaf pans and allow to cool. Refrigerate overnight. Slice and serve with crackers or croutons.

PREP TIME: 3 hours   MAKES: 3 loaf pans

NOTES

_____

_____

_____

_____

_____

_____

COCHON DE LAIT—OVEN-STYLE

The Cochon de lait is described in Louisiana as the art of cooking a pig over an open pecan wood fire. Although the origin of this social event is obscure, it is known that the custom began at least a century ago in Bayou Country. The Germans, settling St. James Parish in 1690, brought with them the pigs and skilled butchers necessary for this art. However, history tells us that the traditional preparation of cochon de lait, French for suckling pig, came to South Louisiana in the early 1800s with veterans of Napoleon's army, who settled in Mansura, Louisiana. Today, Mansura is known as the Cochon de Lait Capital of the World.

METHOD:

Have your butcher prepare a 15-20 pound suckling pig to oven-ready. Place the pig in a roasting pan with 2-inch high sides. Season the pig well inside and out, using salt, cracked black pepper, granulated garlic, thyme, basil and sage. Over-season the outside of the pig, due to the thickness of the skin, only a portion of this seasoning will affect the taste. You may wish to stuff the pig with your favorite rice or cornbread dressing. Do not over-stuff, as stuffing will expand slightly during cooking. Should you wish to stuff, use 4-inch skewers and truss the belly cavity, tying securely with butcher's twine. Place the front feet under the head and the back feet under the belly in the roasting pan. Using a very sharp paring knife, cut diagonal slits at 2-inch intervals in the skin from head to tail. These cuts should be approximately one-eighth inch deep and will enhance the cooking by naturally basting the pig, but will also enhance carving. Place a carrot or a small block of wood in the mouth. Wrap the ears, nose and tail in aluminum foil to prevent over-cooking. Surround the pig with new potatoes, turned carrots, diced celery, onions and apples. Cover the entire pan with aluminum foil and place in a preheated 350 degree F oven. Cook 15 minutes per pound and baste every 30-40 minutes with the natural drippings. When the internal temperature reaches 150 degrees F, the pig is cooked. Remove the foil and allow the skin to brown evenly. Remove pig from oven and place on a large silver tray or serving platter and garnish with oven-browned potatoes and carrots. You may wish to create a natural sauce by deglazing the cooking pan with 2 cups of red wine and 1 cup of beef consomme, found in your local store. You can do so by boiling the wine and beef stock in the cooking pan, while scraping all of the natural drippings that settled to the bottom during cooking. Once this mixture is reduced and thickened, strain it through a fine colander and keep warm for service. Ladle off excess oil before service. Replace the block of wood in the pig's mouth with a red or green apple and place one cherry in each eye. For additional color, you may wish to add a bunch of whole parsley and orange slices around the tray. To carve, remove rear hams first. Slice all meat from these pieces and proceed in the same manner with the front legs. Remove the tenderloins last by inserting a boning knife down each side of the backbone, through the skin, and cutting away this most tender cut of the suckling pig.

PREP TIME: 4-6 hours   SERVES: 8-10

NOTES

_____

_____

_____

_____

_____

_____

ORANGE PORK CHOPS

INGREDIENTS:

2 cups orange juice

1 orange, sectioned

4 center-cut pork chops, 1-inch thick

1 cup flour

$1/4$ cup oil

1 tbsp sugar

$1/8$ tsp nutmeg

2 tbsps raisins

salt and black pepper

Louisiana Gold Pepper Sauce

METHOD:

In a cast iron skillet, heat oil over medium-high heat. Season flour using salt and pepper. Season pork chops using salt, pepper and Louisiana Gold. Dredge pork chops in flour and pan fry until golden brown. In a mixing bowl, combine sugar, nutmeg, raisins and orange juice. Pour juice mixture over chops in skillet, cover and simmer 45 minutes to 1 hour. Place orange sections on top of pork chops, cover and cook an additional 10 minutes. Serve warm with rice or noodles.

PREP TIME: 1 hour   SERVES: 4

NOTES

_____

_____

_____

_____

_____

_____

PORK & TURNIP STEW

INGREDIENTS:

6 center-cut pork chops, 1-inch thick

6 small turnips

1 cup oil

1 cup flour

1 cup chopped onion

$^1\!/_2$ cup chopped celery

$^1\!/_4$ cup chopped bell pepper

$^1\!/_4$ cup diced garlic

2 quarts chicken stock or water

2 cups sliced carrots

$^1\!/_2$ cup sliced green onions

$^1\!/_4$ cup chopped parsley

salt and black pepper

Louisiana Gold Pepper Sauce

METHOD:

In a 7-quart cast iron dutch oven, heat oil over medium-high heat. Season pork chops using salt, pepper and Louisiana Gold. Pan fry pork chops until golden brown on both sides. Remove and keep warm. Sprinkle flour into dutch oven and, using a wire whisk, stir constantly until brown roux is achieved. Add onions, celery, bell pepper and garlic. Saute 3-5 minutes or until vegetables are wilted. Return chops to the dutch oven and add stock or water. Cover dutch oven, decrease temperature to medium and allow to cook until meat is tender, approximately $1^1\!/_2$ hours. Peel turnips and cut into 1-inch cubes. Add turnips to dutch oven, adding more stock or water, if necessary, to retain stew-like consistency. Cook on medium heat until turnips and carrots are tender, approximately $^1\!/_2$ hour. Add green onions and parsley and season to taste using salt, pepper and Louisiana Gold. Serve with steamed white rice and corn bread.

PREP TIME: $2^1\!/_2$ hours   SERVES: 6

NOTES

_____

_____

_____

_____

_____

_____

WHITE BEAN & TASSO SOUP

INGREDIENTS:

1 pound dried white beans
$^1/_2$ pound cubed tasso
1 cup shortening or bacon drippings
1 cup chopped onions
$^1/_2$ cup chopped celery
$^1/_2$ cup chopped bell pepper
$^1/_4$ cup diced garlic

3 quarts water
1 bay leaf
$^1/_2$ cup sliced green onions
$^1/_4$ cup chopped parsley
salt and black pepper
Louisiana Gold Pepper Sauce

METHOD:

The cooking time of the beans will be cut about $^1/_3$ if the beans are soaked overnight in cold water to soften the outer shell. In a 5-quart cast iron dutch oven, melt shortening or bacon drippings over medium-high heat. Add onions, celery, bell peppers, garlic and tasso. Saute approximately 5-10 minutes or until vegetables are wilted. Add drained beans, blending well with vegetables and cook 2-3 minutes. Add bay leaf and enough cold water to cover beans by approximately 2-3 inches. Bring to a rolling boil and allow to cook 10 minutes, stirring occasionally to avoid scorching. Reduce heat to simmer and cook approximately 2 hours or until beans are tender. Stir from time to time, as beans will settle to the bottom of the pot as they cook. When beans are tender, add green onions and parsley. Season to taste using salt, pepper and Louisiana Gold. Using a metal spoon, mash approximately $^1/_3$ of the beans against the side of the pot to create a creaming effect. Once beans are tender and creamy, they are ready to serve. In order for maximum flavor to develop, this dish should be cooked one day prior to serving.

PREP TIME: 2 hours   SERVES: 6

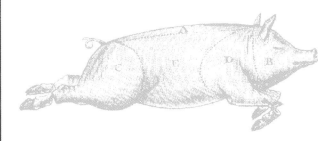

NOTES

_____
_____
_____
_____
_____
_____

Chapter Four
June

Bayou Lacombe Crab Festival

Creole Tomato Festival

Louisiana Blueberry Festival

Louisiana Peach Festival

Poke Salot Festival

BAYOU LACOMBE CRAB FESTIVAL
Lacombe, Louisiana

The blue crab in all of its forms, from soft shell to spicy boiled, is the featured star during the last weekend each June in the small village of Lacombe on the north shore of Lake Ponchartrain. Since 1977, the Bayou Lacombe Crab Festival has entertained thousands and supported many non-profit organizations with festival proceeds.

On the meandering banks of Bayou Lacombe, this festival draws multitudes of festival lovers to the scenic village of 5,000 residents to enjoy crab delicacies which include Soft Shell Crab Poboys, a festival favorite if you judge by the long lines; Crab Seafood Balls, Boiled Crabs and Stuffed Crabs. Other festival favorites include Alligator on a Stick, Crawfish Fettucine, Jambalaya and Gumbo. You will certainly not go hungry at this festival.

In the shade of centuries old live oaks, continuous entertainment can be found and heard for three days straight. You will find musical groups, dancing, kiddie contests such as watermelon eating and bubble gum blowing, games, arts and crafts, and carnival rides. Be sure to visit the country museum located next to the festival grounds.

Selected as one of the top 20 events from nine states by the Southeast Tourism Society, the Bayou Lacombe Crab Festival is an old fashioned, rural celebration for the entire family that you will certainly want to join in.

Lagniappe

The village of Lacombe is conveniently located midway between the cities of Slidell and Mandeville on the north shore of Lake Ponchartrain. It is easily reached by several interstates. While visiting the festival, a stay at any of the following bed-and-breakfasts are a must. The Magnolia House in Madisonville, Windy Pines or Pollyana in Mandeville or The Covington bed-and-breakfast in nearby Madisonville is always a great choice. For dining in Covington, Chef Kim Kringlie's Dakota Restaurant specializes in Cajun and Creole specialties and is open for lunch and dinner. In Lacombe away from the festival grounds, try Sal and Judy's for Italian cuisine and La Provence for Provencal French cuisine. The city of jazz, New Orleans, is just south of Lake Ponchartrain within easy driving distance from the festival. If your point of interest is wild life, make sure you visit the Global Wild Life Center 15 miles west of Covington off Interstate 12. Travel in a covered wagon of a 900 acre home to view many rare, endangered and extinct wild animals from all over the world.

Travel easily to Lacombe from any direction via Interstates 10, 12, 59 or 55. It is situated on Highway 190 between Mandeville and Slidell. For more information about the festival, call the Bayou Lacombe Crab Festival Commission at (504) 882-5528.

Photo: Bill Castel, Heritage Photography
Cultus Pearson and Chef John Folse with a platter of crabs.

TWIN CRABMEATS ETOUFFEE

INGREDIENTS:

1 pound jumbo lump crabmeat
1/2 pound claw crabmeat
1/4 pound butter
1 cup chopped onions
1 cup chopped celery
1/2 cup chopped green bell pepper
1/2 cup chopped red bell pepper
1/2 cup diced tomatoes
2 tbsps diced garlic

2 bay leaves
1/2 cup tomato sauce
1 cup flour
2 quarts crawfish stock or water
1 ounce sherry
1 cup chopped green onions
1/2 cup chopped parsley
salt and black pepper
dash of Louisiana Gold Pepper Sauce

METHOD:

In a 5-quart cast iron dutch oven, melt butter over medium-high heat. Add onions, celery, bell peppers, tomatoes, garlic and bay leaves. Saute 3-5 minutes or until vegetables are wilted. Add claw crabmeat and tomato sauce, blending well into mixture. Using a wire whip, blend flour into the vegetable mixture to form a white roux. Slowly add crawfish stock or water, a little at a time, until all is incorporated. Bring to a low boil, reduce to simmer and cook 15 minutes, stirring occasionally. Add sherry, green onions and parsley and cook an additional 5 minutes. Add jumbo lump crabmeat and season to taste using salt and pepper. Serve in patty shells or over angel hair pasta, spicing with a few dashes of Louisiana Gold.

PREP TIME: 1 hour   SERVES: 6

NOTES

_____
_____
_____
_____
_____
_____

LUMP CRABMEAT AU GRATIN

INGREDIENTS:

2 pounds jumbo lump crabmeat
$^1/_4$ pound butter
$^1/_4$ cup diced onions
$^1/_4$ cup diced celery
$^1/_4$ cup chopped red bell pepper
$^1/_4$ cup chopped yellow bell pepper
$^1/_4$ cup chopped green bell pepper
1 tbsp diced garlic
3 tbsps flour

$3^1/_2$ cups hot whipping cream
1 ounce dry white wine
1 tbsp lemon juice
$^1/_2$ cup grated cheddar cheese
$^1/_4$ cup sliced green onions
$^1/_4$ cup chopped parsley
salt and cracked black pepper
Louisiana Gold Pepper Sauce

METHOD:

Preheat oven to 375 degrees F. In a 3-quart cast iron dutch oven, melt butter over medium-high heat. Add onions, celery, red, yellow and green bell peppers and garlic. Saute 3-5 minutes or until vegetables are wilted. Be careful not to brown vegetables. Sprinkle in flour, blending well into mixture. Using a wire whip, whisk hot cream into dutch oven, stirring constantly until a thick cream sauce is achieved. Reduce heat to simmer, add white wine and lemon juice to hot sauce. Sprinkle in half of the cheddar cheese, stirring the mixture constantly. Season to taste using salt, pepper and Louisiana Gold. Add green onions and parsley for color. If mixture becomes too thick, add a small amount of hot water or whipping cream. Place equal parts of jumbo lump crab in six au gratin dishes, top with sauce and sprinkle with remaining cheddar cheese. Bake for 10 minutes or until cheese is bubbly.

PREP TIME: 45 minutes   SERVES: 6

NOTES

_____

_____

_____

_____

_____

_____

PAN-FRIED SOFTSHELL CRAB

INGREDIENTS FOR BATTER:

½ cup milk

1 cup water

1 egg

3 tbsps Creole mustard

1 tsp fresh thyme, chopped

1 tsp fresh basil, chopped

1 tsp fresh dill, chopped

salt and black pepper

Louisiana Gold Pepper Sauce

METHOD FOR BATTER:

In a 1-quart mixing bowl, combine all of the above ingredients. Whisk with a wire whip to ensure mixture is well blended. Set aside.

INGREDIENTS FOR BREADING:

2 cups corn flour

2¼ tsps salt

1½ tsps granulated garlic

1½ tsps black pepper

1½ tsps cayenne pepper

1½ tsps dry thyme

METHOD FOR BREADING:

In a 1-quart mixing bowl, combine all of the above ingredients. Set aside.

INGREDIENTS FOR FRYING:

6 jumbo softshell crabs

2 cups vegetable oil

METHOD FOR FRYING:

Preheat oven to 250 degrees F. In a 10-inch cast iron skillet, preheat one cup of oil over medium-high heat to 325 degrees F. Place softshell crab in batter mixture, drain thoroughly and bread in the corn flour mixture. Shake off all excess breading and pan saute, a few crabs at a time, turning frequently until golden brown on all sides. Remove, drain on paper towels and keep warm in oven. Additional oil may be added to the skillet, as needed, during the saute process. Serve the crabs hot with tartar or cocktail sauce.

*NOTE: Yellow corn flour may be found in most gourmet shops or food stores. It may be found packaged and pre-seasoned as a seafood breading mix such as Zatarain's Fish Fry. If unavailable in your area, plain flour or equal parts of flour and yellow corn meal may be substituted.

PREP TIME: 30 minutes   SERVES: 6

NOTES

_____

_____

_____

_____

_____

_____

BAYOU LACOMBE CRAB BOULETTES

INGREDIENTS:

1 pound white crabmeat
$\frac{1}{2}$ cup vegetable oil
$\frac{1}{4}$ cup minced onions
$\frac{1}{4}$ cup minced celery
$\frac{1}{4}$ cup minced red bell pepper
1 tbsp chopped garlic

$\frac{1}{4}$ cup sliced green onions
2 whole eggs
2 cups seasoned Italian bread crumbs
salt and black pepper
Louisiana Gold Pepper Sauce

METHOD:

It is important to pick through the crabmeat to remove any shells. In a 1-gallon cast iron dutch oven, heat vegetable oil to 350 degrees F. In a large mixing bowl, combine all ingredients except bread crumbs, salt, pepper and Louisiana Gold. Using a wooden spoon, blend thoroughly. Sprinkle in enough bread crumbs to hold the mixture together, but make sure dressing is not too bready. Season to taste using salt, pepper and Louisiana Gold. Roll the boulettes into 1-inch balls, sprinkle with remaining bread crumbs and fry until golden brown. Serve as an hors d'oeuvre or as an addition to pasta sauce or etouffee.

PREP TIME: 30 minutes   MAKES: 20

CRAB FINGERS ROCKEFELLER

INGREDIENTS:

1 pound cleaned crab fingers
$1\frac{1}{2}$ cups extra virgin olive oil
$\frac{1}{2}$ cup red wine vinegar
1 tbsp Creole mustard
1 tbsp chopped garlic
$\frac{1}{4}$ cup chopped parsley

$\frac{1}{4}$ cup fresh tarragon, chopped
$\frac{1}{4}$ cup sliced green onions
salt and black pepper
Louisiana Gold Pepper Sauce
$\frac{1}{4}$ cup minced carrots

METHOD:

In the bottom of a large ceramic mixing bowl, combine all ingredients except crab claws. Whisk vigorously until all ingredients are well blended. Place the crab claws into a 1-quart mason jar and top with the Rockefeller marinade. Screw on top tightly and turn the jar upside down, two to three times, to coat the claws well. Place in the refrigerator overnight, turning every few hours. The longer the claws stand in the marinade, the more intense the flavor. When ready to serve, pour the contents of the jar onto a decorative serving platter and garnish with lemon slices.

PREP TIME: 1 hour   SERVES: 6

NOTES

_____

_____

_____

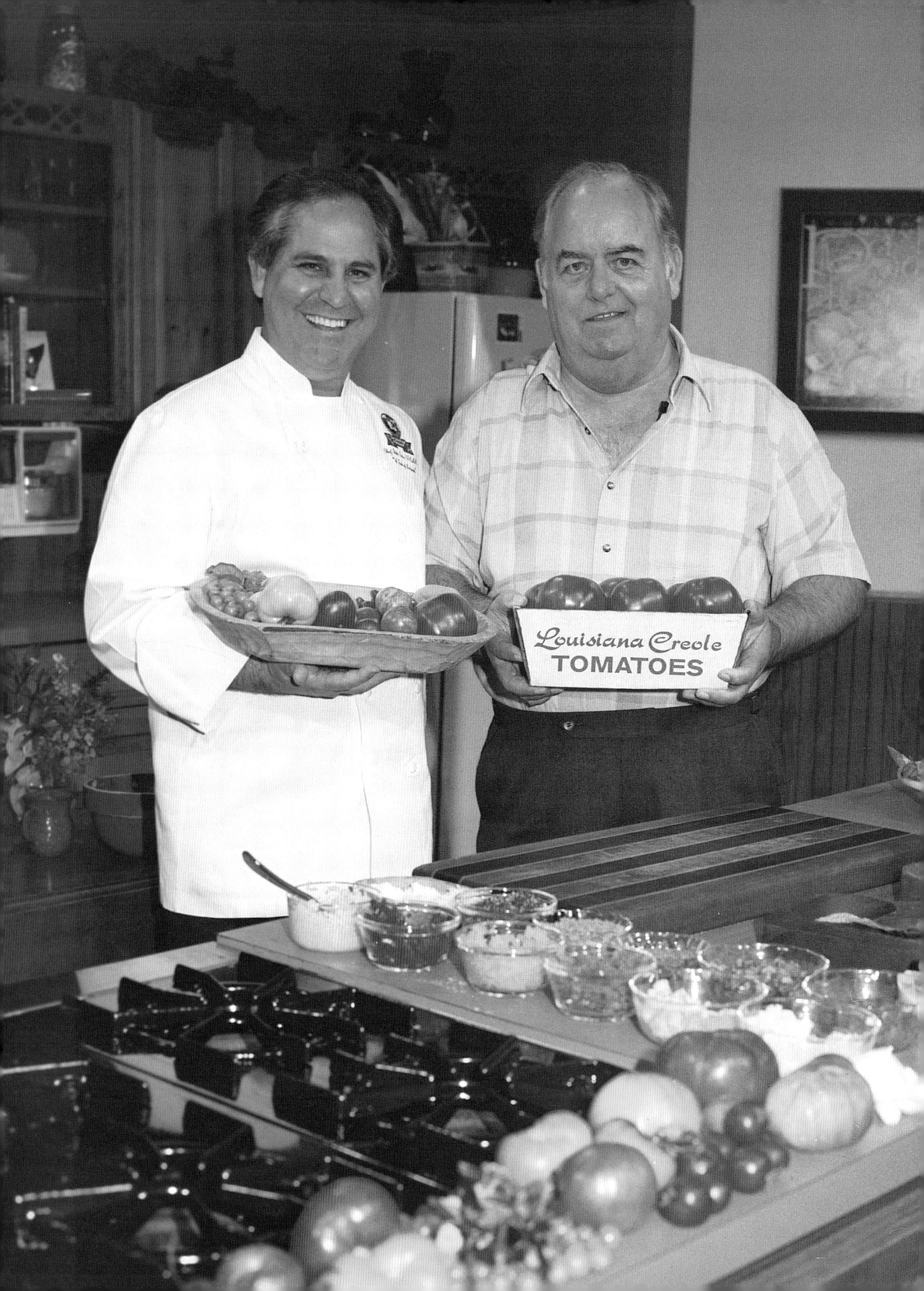
Louisiana Creole
TOMATOES

CREOLE TOMATO FESTIVAL
French Market, New Orleans, Louisiana

On the first weekend each June, the City of New Orleans rolls out the red carpet to over 50,000 locals and visitors as it celebrates the start of the home-grown vegetable season during its Creole Tomato Festival in the historic French Market.

South Louisianians have developed thousands of dishes to feature this variety of the popular fruit (not vegetable), defined as one that is bigger, sweeter, juicier and meatier than those grown anywhere else in the world. After nurturing this appetizing variety in their home gardens, picking only when red-ripe, the locals are just as quick eat the Creole Tomatoes out-of-hand as they are to impart their zest into countless tantalizing dishes.

Served fried and topped with crawfish, smothered with okra and shrimp, or just prepared in a bisque or gumbo, the luscious, juicy and ripe Creole Tomato is the subject of conversation and the featured star during this annual fest. Amidst street performers and live jazz bands atop stages throughout the market, celebrity chefs offer samples of their favorite dishes, along with the recipes, to the participants. After the sampling, a cold Bloody Mary is in order.

More than just a setting for the exciting festival, the French Market is alive with shopping and entertainment opportunities after two hundred years of business. The stalls of the Farmers' Market are filled with ripe, meaty Creole Tomatoes and the farmers have been known to boast about why their tomatoes are best as they beckon shoppers with a shout of, "Get the best ripe and juicy Creole tomatoes here." And, who will want to miss that world-famous establishment serving up its coffee and beignets, Cafe Du Monde.

After enjoying the festival, visitors will also want to explore the Vieux Carre, or French Quarter, where the sounds of jazz fill the streets day and night. Its Old World architecture is perfectly set in narrow cobblestone streets, where one may peek through the wrought-iron gates to see lush tropical gardens. Antique shops, book stalls, and art galleries abound while painters, sculptors, jewelers and artisans of all sorts line the streets.

Lagniappe

There are hundreds of restaurants in the Quarter, but a meal at famed Antoine's, Brennan's, Emeril's, Bayona's, K- Paul's or Uglesich's Restaurant is a must. Lodging options range from the classic elegance of the Royal Sonesta Hotel to a multitude of quaint bed-and-breakfast establishments such as the 14-room Corn Stalk Hotel. Beyond the French Quarter, an endless variety of entertainment is available. Families will want to visit the Aquarium of the Americas and the Audubon Zoo and Botanical Gardens. A riverboat cruise down the mighty Mississippi River is a sure winner; and if you want to see the legendary Louisiana alligators, take one of the many swamp tours offered. Build a weekend around this distinctive festival and partake of the sites, sounds and, of course, flavors of the internationally-famous city of fine cuisine and culture.

Exit I-10 at Canal Street, travel to Decatur Street, and enter the French Quarter. The festival covers five blocks of North Peters Street from Cafe Du Monde to the Farmers' Market. Admission is free. Call (504) 522-2621.

Photo: Bill Castel, Heritage Photography
Chef John Folse with Sam Benandi and his world-famous Creole tomatoes.

TOMATO BISQUE

INGREDIENTS:

½ cup olive oil

2 cups chopped onions

1 cup chopped celery

½ cup chopped bell pepper

¼ cup chopped garlic

1 cup diced carrots

1 cup flour

8 medium Creole tomatoes

1 cup tomato sauce

1 cup dry white wine

3 quarts beef stock

1 tbsp fresh basil, chopped

1 tbsp fresh thyme, chopped

1 tbsp fresh oregano, chopped

1 cup whipping cream

1 ½ tsps salt

⅛ tsp white pepper

Louisiana Gold Pepper Sauce

8 leaves fresh basil, cut into strips

METHOD:

Cut tomatoes in half, remove cores and squeeze out seeds. Chop two tomatoes coarsely and reserve for garnish. In a 5-quart cast iron dutch oven, heat olive oil over medium-low heat. Add onions, celery, bell peppers, garlic and carrots. Saute 3-5 minutes or until vegetables are wilted. Sprinkle in flour and, using a wire whisk, blend well into the vegetable mixture. Add tomatoes, tomato sauce and white wine, blending well into the roux mixture. Add beef stock until a soup-like consistency is achieved. Bring to a low boil, reduce to simmer and add basil, thyme and oregano. Cook 30-minutes, adding stock as necessary to retain volume. Fold in cream and season to taste using salt, pepper and Louisiana Gold. When ready to serve, garnish with chopped tomatoes and fresh basil.

PREP TIME: 1½ hours   SERVES: 6-8

NOTES

_____

_____

_____

_____

_____

_____

TOMATO SALAD

INGREDIENTS:

1 Creole tomato

1 orange tomato

1 yellow tomato

1 large Bermuda or red onion

1 tsp fresh basil, chopped

1 tsp fresh oregano, chopped

olive oil

Steen's Cane Vinegar

salt and black pepper

Louisiana Gold Pepper Sauce

METHOD:

Slice tomatoes $\frac{1}{4}$-inch thick. Slice onion $\frac{1}{8}$-inch thick and separate. On a 10-inch platter, arrange sliced tomatoes and top with onions. Sprinkle on fresh basil and oregano. Top with olive oil and vinegar. Season to taste using salt, pepper and Louisiana Gold.

PREP TIME: 30 Minutes   SERVES: 4

FRIED GREEN TOMATOES

INGREDIENTS:

3 green tomatoes

1 $\frac{1}{2}$ cups oil

1 cup flour

1 cup seasoned Italian bread crumbs

1 cup milk

1 egg

1 cup water

salt and black pepper

1 tbsp chopped basil

Louisiana Gold Pepper Sauce

METHOD:

In a 10-inch cast iron skillet, heat oil to 350 degrees F. Slice tomatoes $\frac{1}{2}$-inch thick and drain on a paper towel. Season flour with salt and pepper. Add chopped basil to the bread crumbs. Prepare egg wash by combining milk, egg and water. Blend well using a wire whisk. Season to taste using salt, pepper and Louisiana Gold. Dredge tomato slices first in flour, next in egg wash, then in bread crumbs. Pan fry, a few at a time, until golden brown on each side. Remove and drain well. Eat as a salad topped with remoulade or tartar sauce.

PREP TIME: 30 minutes   SERVES: 6

NOTES

_____

_____

_____

_____

_____

_____

CREOLE TOMATO MARINARA WITH CRAWFISH & PASTA

INGREDIENTS FOR SAUCE:

¼ cup olive oil

½ pound crawfish tails

¼ cup slivered garlic

½ cup chopped onions

½ cup chopped celery

½ cup chopped bell pepper

2 cups diced Creole tomatoes

1 cup V-8 or tomato juice

½ cup tomato sauce

1 tbsp fresh basil, chopped

1 tbsp fresh thyme, chopped

1 bay leaf

salt and black pepper

Louisiana Gold Pepper Sauce

METHOD:

Heat olive oil in a cast iron skillet over medium-high heat. Add garlic and saute 1-2 minutes, stirring constantly until golden but not browned. Add onions, celery and bell pepper. Saute 3-5 minutes or until vegetables are wilted. Add tomatoes, V-8 juice and bay leaf. Bring to a low boil, reduce to simmer and cook approximately 7-10 minutes. Add crawfish tails, basil and thyme. Season to taste using salt, pepper and Louisiana Gold. If sauce tastes a little too acidic, you may wish to add a pinch of sugar. When sauce is done, pour over a bed of hot angel hair pasta.

PREP TIME: 1 Hour   SERVES: 6

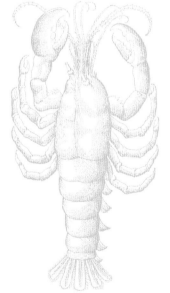

NOTES

_____

_____

_____

_____

_____

PANSANELLA

INGREDIENTS:

3 cups diced Creole tomatoes
2 tbsps chopped fresh basil
1 tsp chopped fresh thyme
$^1/_2$ cup extra virgin olive oil
$^1/_4$ cup red wine vinegar
$^3/_4$ cup grated Parmesan cheese
25 whole basil leaves
25 French bread croutons, toasted
salt and black pepper

METHOD:

In a large mixing bowl, combine all ingredients except whole basil leaves and croutons. Blend well, cover and refrigerate 1-2 hours. When ready to serve, place one whole basil leaf on top of a French bread crouton and serve one heaping tablespoon of the Pansanella on top. Eat as a cold hors d'oeuvre.

PREP TIME: 30 minutes   SERVES: 4

NOTES

_____

_____

_____

_____

_____

_____

BLUEBERRY FESTIVAL
Mansfield, Louisiana

In Desoto Parish, an area of north Louisiana bordering Texas, there are over a dozen blueberry farms which flourish in the mid-summer months. It is the result of a two-acre patch of blueberries planted by an 80-year-old couple more than a decade ago. They paved the way for the Parish's now famous blueberry industry which is celebrated in grand style each June, in the heart of blueberry season, in Mansfield, Louisiana.

The farms which now dot the parish yield more than 1 million pounds of blueberries annually, making this area the largest blueberry producer in the state. It was only a few years ago that the blueberry was considered one of Louisiana's newest fruit crops, but with the successful spread of early and late ripening varieties, this crop is growing strong. The locals have put them to good use in a wide variety of tantalizing recipes including blueberry drinks, syrups, butter, breads, pies, pastries and toppings.

All of the recipes featuring the deep blue berries can be sampled at the festival, and don't forget that festival favorite — fried blueberry pies. The baking contest is also a popular attraction. As with many of the Louisiana fairs and festivals, you will find that unique gift or souvenir as you browse through over a hundred exhibits of arts and crafts.

The festival is held in scenic downtown Mansfield around the Courthouse Square. Join the thousands who come out to north Louisiana in June to enjoy the festivities featuring this succulent, cool blue treat. You can even go out and pick your own if you like.

Lagniappe

While in Mansfield, you will want to tour the historic homes and churches in the area. Sites include Rock Chapel in Carmel, the Grand Cane Methodist Church, built in 1988, and Rockwood Gardens. Mansfield was the site of a decisive Civil War battle. Union General Nathaniel Banks engaged numerous battles against the Confederacy in and around this area which gives this town a real historical twist. You may consider a stay at the local Mansfield Inn and a hot meal at Camellia Grill. Mansfield is located only 30 miles south of the city of Shreveport.

Travel on I-49 and exit Highway 84. Travel west to Mansfield. For more information on the festival, call the Mansfield Chamber of Commerce at (318) 872-1310.

Photo: Bill Castel, Heritage Photography
Chef John Folse and Tom Avant. Clockwise from bottom left: Blueberry Cornbread-Stuffed Game Hen, Blueberries 'N Cream Cheesecake, Blueberry Zucchini Bread and Blueberry Lemon Pound Cake.

BLUEBERRY ZUCCHINI BREAD

INGREDIENTS:

2 cups blueberries

3 eggs, beaten

2 cups sugar

1 cup vegetable oil

1 tsp vanilla

2 cups grated zucchini

3$\frac{1}{2}$ cups self-rising flour

1 tsp cinnamon

1 cup chopped pecans

METHOD:

Preheat oven to 350 degrees F. Grease two 9"x 5"x 3" loaf pans and set aside. In a large mixing bowl, combine eggs, sugar, oil and vanilla. Using a wire whisk, blend well. Stir in zucchini until it is well blended into the egg mixture. Slowly add flour, stirring into the liquids until all is incorporated. Add cinnamon, pecans and blueberries. Gently fold into the batter and, when thoroughly mixed, spoon into the loaf pan and bake for approximately 45 minutes or until thoroughly cooked. Cool in pans for 5 minutes then remove to a wire rack. For best flavor, serve warm.

PREP TIME: 1$\frac{1}{2}$ hours   MAKES: 2 loaves

BLUEBERRY SAUCE

INGREDIENTS:

$\frac{2}{3}$ cup sugar

2 tbsps corn starch

pinch of nutmeg

pinch of cinnamon

1 cup water

2 cups fresh blueberries

2 tbsps lemon juice

METHOD:

In a small sauce pot, combine sugar, corn starch, nutmeg and cinnamon. Gradually stir in water and cook over medium heat until mixture boils and thickens. Fold in fresh blueberries and lemon juice. Cook 10-15 minutes or until sauce is rich and full-colored. Cool slightly. Serve warm over ice cream or dessert. A tablespoon of this mixture may be placed into any natural drippings of duck, venison or lamb to enhance the sauce.

PREP TIME: 30 minutes   MAKES: 2$\frac{1}{4}$ cups

NOTES

_____

_____

_____

_____

_____

_____

BLUEBERRY LEMON POUND CAKE

INGREDIENTS:

1 cup fresh blueberries
1 lemon rind, grated
6 tbsps butter
1¹/₂ cups sugar
2 eggs
1¹/₂ cups flour

1 tbsp baking powder
2 tsps flour
pinch of salt
¹/₂ cup milk
3 tsps fresh lemon juice

METHOD:

Preheat oven to 350 degrees F. Grease an 8" x 4" loaf pan and set aside. In a mixing bowl, cream butter and 1 cup of sugar. Beat on medium speed until well blended. Add eggs, one at a time, blending thoroughly into the mixture. In a separate bowl, combine 1¹/₂ cups flour, baking powder and salt. Slowly add flour to the sugar mixture, alternately with milk, while constantly stirring. Dredge blueberries in remaining 2 teaspoons of flour. Fold into the batter, along with the lemon rind. Pour batter into loaf pan and bake for approximately 1 hour or until thoroughly cooked. Combine remaining 1/2 cup sugar and lemon juice into a small sauce pan over medium-high heat until totally dissolved. When cake is done, remove from oven and pierce the top at even intervals with a toothpick. Pour the lemon mixture over the top of the cake and allow to cool.

PREP TIME: 2 hours   SERVES: 8

NOTES

_____
_____
_____
_____
_____
_____

BLUEBERRIES 'N CREAM CHEESECAKE

INGREDIENTS:

2$\frac{1}{2}$ cups fresh blueberries

3 (8-ounce) packages cream cheese, softened

1 cup sugar

5 eggs

3 tbsps corn starch

$\frac{1}{4}$ tsp salt

1$\frac{1}{2}$ cups sour cream

2 tbsps sugar

$\frac{1}{2}$ tsp vanilla extract

$\frac{1}{4}$ cup sugar

$\frac{1}{4}$ cup water

1 cup fresh blueberries

METHOD:

Preheat oven to 325 degrees F. Grease a 9-inch springform pan and set aside. Combine 2$\frac{1}{2}$ cups blueberries with 1 tablespoon of corn starch. Place in the bowl of a food processor and puree until smooth. Place pureed mixture into a cast iron skillet over medium-high heat and cook until slightly thickened, approximately 5 minutes. Remove from heat and cool. Reserve $\frac{1}{2}$ cup of blueberry puree for glaze. Into the bowl of an electric mixer, place cream cheese and 1 cup of sugar. Beat until light and fluffy. Add eggs, one at a time, beating well after each addition. Stir in remaining 2 tablespoons of corn starch and salt. Pour batter into springform pan. Pour puree into cheesecake batter in a stream and gently swirl with a knife or toothpick to create a marbling affect. Bake for 45 minutes or until set. Remove from oven and cool on wire rack for 20 minutes. In a mixing bowl, combine sour cream, 2 tablespoons of sugar and vanilla. Mix well to incorporate all ingredients. Spread mixture over cheesecake and bake for 10 additional minutes. Cool cheesecake on wire rack, cover and chill for 8 hours. In a 10-inch cast iron skillet, combine reserved $\frac{1}{2}$ cup puree, $\frac{1}{4}$ cup sugar and water. Cook over medium heat, stirring constantly, until thickened. Gently fold in remaining 1 cup blueberries and allow to cool. Remove cake from pan and spoon on glaze when serving.

PREP TIME: 1$\frac{1}{2}$ hours   SERVES: 8

NOTES

_____

_____

_____

_____

_____

_____

BLUEBERRY CORNBREAD STUFFED GAME HEN

INGREDIENTS:

6 Rock Cornish Game hens
2 cups fresh blueberries
1 cup orange juice
$1/4$ pound butter
$1/2$ pound bulk sausage
2 cups diced onions
$1/4$ cup diced celery
$1/4$ cup diced red bell pepper
$1/4$ cup diced garlic
$1/2$ cup diced apples
4 cups cooked corn bread
$1/4$ cup chopped parsley

$1/4$ cup sliced green onions
1 tsp fresh sage, chopped
$1/2$ tsp fresh thyme, chopped
$1/2$ tsp fresh rosemary, chopped
salt and black pepper
granulated garlic
Louisiana Gold Pepper Sauce
3 cups chicken stock
$1/2$ cup chopped pecans
1 cup dry sherry
$1/2$ cup melted butter

METHOD:

Preheat oven to 350 degrees F. Rinse cornish hens under cold running water. Drain well. Place the cornish hens in a large cast iron dutch oven and sprinkle with the orange juice. Season generously, inside and out, using salt, pepper, granulated garlic and Louisiana Gold. In a cast iron skillet, melt $1/4$ pound of butter over medium-high heat. Add bulk sausage and cook until brown. Add onions, celery, bell pepper and garlic. Saute 3-5 minutes or until vegetables are wilted. Add apples, blending well into the sausage mixture. When apples are slightly cooked, pour the mixture into a large mixing bowl. Add blueberries, corn bread, parsley, green onions, sage, thyme and rosemary. Using a wooden spoon, fold the corn bread into the sausage mixture. Add two cups of chicken stock or enough to moisten the corn bread and hold the stuffing together. Add pecans and season to taste using salt and pepper. Stuff the cornish hens with equal amounts of the stuffing, placing any excess stuffing in the corners of the roasting pan. Top the hens with sherry and melted butter. Bake, uncovered, for approximately one hour, basting the hens frequently during the process. When hens are golden brown, remove them from the oven and serve with natural pan drippings.

PREP TIME: $1^1/2$ hours   SERVES: 6

NOTES

_____
_____
_____
_____
_____
_____

PEACH FESTIVAL
Ruston, Louisiana

Louisianians know that a peach just isn't a peach unless it is grown in Ruston. As the hub of Lincoln Parish in north Louisiana along Interstate 20, Ruston is undoubtedly the place to find the ripest, juiciest, sweetest peaches. Georgia . . . well, we prefer our home-grown varieties.

Peaches are harvested from May through August. Although each variety has a harvest period of only two weeks, the wide number of species extends the harvest season through the summer. It is during this peak harvest period that this north Louisiana town celebrates its famous crop by hosting the Louisiana Peach Festival. The locals have been celebrating this festival since the early 1950s and have built quite a tradition.

During the festivities you can check out the many great dishes at one of the featured events, the Peach Cookery Contest. Many versions of Peach Cobbler and Peach Pie have been among the Grand Champion winners of this contest. The Peach Cookbook is also a great keepsake from this festival, and cooking demonstrations are a big hit with the festival-goers.

Don't miss the Peach Festival Parade, another highlight. And, as with most Louisiana festivals, the best crafters are on hand at the Arts and Crafts Fair to show and sell their work.

Everything in Ruston is coming up "peachy" for this festival. Attending the festival is a great reason to visit this beautiful part of Louisiana, dubbed "Sportsman's Paradise."

Lagniappe

Ruston, Louisiana in located in north Louisiana along I-20. It is the hub of Lincoln Parish, an area filled with many family activities. Whether you prefer outdoor activities such as boating, fishing or mountain-bike riding; shopping for antiques; or simply sampling down-home cooking, Lincoln Parish is the place for you. From a great meal at Sarah's Kitchen to a stay at one of the seven hotels, bed-and-breakfast establishments or new RV facilities, you will feel right at home in Ruston. Melody Hills Ranch, 5 miles from Ruston, is a good choice for lodging. Ruston is centrally located between the north Louisiana cities of Shreveport to the west and Monroe to the east. You may wish to visit the town of Arcadia, famous because it's the site where Bonnie and Clyde met their fate at the hands of lawmen.

Travel on I-20 to Ruston. For more information about the festival, call the Ruston/Lincoln Convention and Visitors Bureau at (318) 255-2031.

Photo: Bill Castel, Heritage Photography
Chef John Folse and Joe Mitcham. Clockwise from bottom left: Roasted Loin Chops in Peach and Persimmon Glaze, Peach Cobbler, Peach Trifle

FRENCH PEACH PIE

INGREDIENTS:

9 or 10 fresh peaches

$^1/_3$ cup sugar

2 tbsps flour

1 cup milk

3 egg yolks

1 tbsp butter

1 tsp vanilla

1 tbsp lemon juice

2 tbsps butter

2 tbsps sugar

$^1/_4$ tsp nutmeg

$^1/_4$ tsp cinnamon

$^1/_2$ cup peach preserves

1 egg yolk, whipped

2 (9-inch) pie shells

METHOD:

Preheat oven to 425 degrees F. Press one 9-inch pie shell into the bottom of a pie pan. Set aside. Into a cast iron pot, combine $^1/_3$ cup of sugar, flour, milk and 3 egg yolks. Using a wire whisk, beat until well blended. Place on medium-high heat until sauce thickens, but do not boil. Remove from heat and whisk in 1 tablespoon of butter and vanilla. Pour the mixture into a bowl and set aside to cool. Peel peaches and cut into $^1/_2$-inch slices. Sprinkle with lemon juice and set aside. In a 10-inch cast iron skillet, melt remaining 2 tablespoons of butter over medium-high heat. Add peaches, 2 tablespoons of sugar and nutmeg. Saute 5 minutes or until peaches are slightly cooked. Remove from heat and allow peaches to cool slightly. Pour peaches into prepared pie pan and top with custard sauce. Spoon peach preserves evenly over the custard and top with second pie shell. Crimp the edges in a decorative fashion and, using a paring knife, cut 4 steam holes into the top shell. Brush evenly with whipped egg yolk and bake 30-45 minutes or until golden brown.

PREP TIME: 1$^1/_2$ hours   SERVES: 6

NOTES

_____

_____

_____

_____

_____

_____

PEACH NUT BREAD

INGREDIENTS:

2 cups peeled peaches, chopped
3 eggs
2 tsps vanilla
1 cup sugar
1 cup oil
$^1/_4$ tsp baking powder

1 tsp baking soda
3 cups flour
1 tsp salt
3 tsps cinnamon
1 cup chopped nuts

METHOD:

Preheat oven to 350 degrees F. Grease two 9"x 4" loaf pans. Place eggs in a large mixing bowl. Using a wire whisk, beat until light and fluffy. Add vanilla, sugar and oil, stirring well to incorporate. Add peaches and blend well into the egg mixture. Sift together dry ingredients and stir into peaches. Fold in nuts and blend well. Pour into bread pans and bake for 1 hour.

PREP TIME: $1^1/_2$ hours   SERVES: 6

PEACH TRIFLE

INGREDIENTS:

3 cups sliced peaches
1 package peach gelatin
1 cup boiling water
1 package lady fingers

$1^1/_2$ cups cold milk
1 (8-ounce) box vanilla instant pudding
2/3 cup sugar
1 (12 ounce) container Cool Whip

METHOD:

In a blender or food processor, blend gelatin and one cup of boiling water. Allow mixture to cool in blender for 1 hour or until slightly thickened but not totally set. Line a 10-inch trifle bowl with lady fingers. In a large mixing bowl, combine milk and pudding. Pour pudding over lady fingers and place in refrigerator until set. Into cooled gelatin, add sugar and peaches. Blend well to incorporate all ingredients. Pour half of the gelatin/peach mixture over the pudding layer and lady fingers. Mix remaining gelatin/peach mixture with half of the Cool Whip and pour over peach mixture. Spoon in remaining Cool Whip and decorate with additional peach slices.

PREP TIME: 45 minutes   SERVES: 6-8

NOTES

_____

_____

_____

_____

_____

_____

ROASTED LOIN CHOPS IN PEACH & PERSIMMON GLAZE

INGREDIENTS:

1 (4-pound) pork loin, bone-in
2 cups sliced peaches
1 cup diced persimmons or red grapes
1/4 cup vegetable oil
1 cup diced Vidalia onions
1 cup diced celery
1/4 cup whole garlic cloves

1 tbsp sliced cayenne or jalapeno peppers
1 quart beef stock
salt and black pepper to taste
2 tbsps rubbed sage
Louisiana Gold Pepper Sauce
1/4 cup chopped mint leaves

METHOD:

Preheat oven to 400 degrees F. You may wish to remove the small flat bones on the backside of the loin which will make the chops easier to slice after cooking. Season the roast well using salt, pepper, sage and Louisiana Gold. Cut slits into the roast to allow salt, pepper and sage to reach the center of the meat. In a cast iron dutch oven, heat oil over medium-high heat. Brown loin well on each side, turning frequently during the browning process. Once browned, add onions, celery, garlic, peaches, persimmons and jalapenos. Pour in stock and bring to a rolling boil. Cover, place in oven and cook until roast is tender, approximately 1 1/2 hours. Remove roast from dutch oven and keep warm. Reduce the pan drippings over medium-high heat until sauce consistency is achieved. If a smooth finish is desired, strain the solid ingredients from the sauce. Slice roast into individual slices and top with sauce. Garnish with chopped mint leaves.

PREP TIME: 2 hours   SERVES: 6-8

NOTES

_____

_____

_____

_____

_____

PEACH COBBLER

INGREDIENTS FOR FILLING:

6 cups fresh peaches, sliced

1$^1/_2$ cups sugar

$^1/_4$ cup water

3 tbsps flour

$^1/_4$ cup sugar

pinch of salt

pinch of cinnamon

pinch of nutmeg

pinch of allspice

$^1/_4$ cup water

INGREDIENTS FOR CRUST:

1 cup all purpose flour

$^1/_2$ cup sugar

2 tsps baking powder

$^1/_2$ tsp salt

$^3/_4$ cup milk

METHOD:

Preheat oven to 400 degrees F. In a cast iron sauce pot, combine peaches, 1 $^1/_2$ cups of sugar and water. Bring to a rolling boil, reduce to simmer and allow fruit to cook until softened. In a measuring cup, blend 3 tablespoons of flour, $^1/_4$ cup of sugar, salt, cinnamon, nutmeg and allspice. Add remaining water and blend well to dissolve flour. Pour into the peach mixture, stirring constantly until mixture thickens. Remove from heat and pour the mixture into a 9-inch cast iron skillet or cobbler pan and allow to cool slightly. In a mixing bowl, combine 1 cup of flour, $^1/_2$ cup of sugar, baking powder, salt and milk. Using a wire whisk, whip until well blended. Pour the batter in an irregular shape over the center of the cobbler and bake for approximately 45 minutes or until golden brown. *NOTE: You may wish to garnish the cobbler with fresh sliced peaches, powdered sugar and a sprig of mint.*

PREP TIME: 1$^1/_2$ hours   SERVES: 8

NOTES

_____

_____

_____

_____

_____

_____

POKE SALOT FESTIVAL
Oak Grove, Louisiana

A trip to North Louisiana in April will lead you to one of the most uniquely-named festivals of the state — the Poke Salot Festival. You are not alone if you are wondering about the origin of this festival's namesake. Since 1986, the streets of Oak Grove have come alive with a celebration of the pokeweed, a little known vegetable which grows abundantly in the South, but is not commercially marketed or even planted. It used to be an important vegetable to country cooks because it grows generously in yards and fields in the spring. Some people find its wild and tender taste the most flavorful of the Southern greens.

The wild weed is prepared in a similar manner to spinach or mustard greens: washed and boiled with simple seasonings occasionally adding smoked meats. It can be found in a variety of recipes at the festival and is sold by the can for those who like it prepared simply.

This curious festival features the Poke Salad Cook Off, a festival highlight, in the Courthouse Square. Here you can discover over 30 dishes featuring the pokeweed as the main ingredient. Entries have included Poke Salad Casserole, Fruitcake and Dips, along with a festival winner, the Poke Salad and Shrimp Egg Rolls.

Family entertainment is plentiful as with most more-traditionally named festivals. There is a circus, petting zoo, and parade, along with carnival rides and good music. A street dance ends the grand celebration of one of Louisiana's most unique foods.

Lagniappe

Oak Grove is located in Louisiana's upper northeast corner, only 19 miles from the Arkansas border. The town population is an estimated 2,500. Lodging and dining is available in the immediate festival area at Mike's Catfish House and Motel, only a few miles west of Oak Grove on Highway 2. You may also want to try a meal at Creech's Restaurant. For entertainment away from the festival, you may want to see the historical Indian Mounds at Poverty Point Commemorative Area or the Louisiana Cotton Museum. A drive to the north Louisiana city of Monroe is 65 miles southwest of Oak Grove.

Travel on I-20, exit at Delhi, travel 30 miles north on Highway 17 to Oak Grove. Alternate route: Travel into Oak Grove on Highway 2 from the west. For more information, call festival organizer Harold Russel at (318) 428-2161.

Editor's Note: "**Poke Salad** " *has various spellings including* **salot, salet** *and* **salad**. *In our recipes, we have chosen to use the common American spelling* **salad**.

Photo: Jose´ L. Garcia, II
Clockwise from bottom left: Poke Salad Cornbread, Poke Salad Lasagna

POKE SALAD DIP

INGREDIENTS:

1 cup poke salad, cooked and drained (or canned)

1½ cups sour cream

2 cups mayonnaise

8 ounces cream cheese, softened

1 cup pecans

1 cup sliced green onions

2 tsps herb-seasoned salt

1½ tsps oregano

1 tsp dried dill weed

juice of 1 lemon

salt and black pepper

1 large red cabbage

"Poke, the <u>Phytolacca</u> <u>americana</u> of the botanists, is probably the best known and most widely used wild vegetable in America. The Indian tribes eagerly sought it and early explorers were unstinting in their praise of this succulent potherb. They carried seeds when they went back home and poke soon became a popular cultivated garden vegetable in southern Europe and North Africa, a position it still maintains. In America it is still a favorite green vegetable with many country people and the tender young sprouts, gathered from wild plants, often appear in vegetable markets, especially in the South." <u>Stalking the Wild Asparagus</u>, Euell Gibbons

METHOD:

In a large mixing bowl, combine poke salad, sour cream, mayonnaise, cream cheese, pecans and green onions. Using a wooden spoon, mix thoroughly until all ingredients are well blended. Add herb seasoning, oregano, dill weed and lemon juice. Season to taste using salt and pepper. Cover bowl with clear wrap and place in refrigerator for a minimum of 2 hours. Trim core end of cabbage to form a flat base. Cut a crosswise slice from the top, making it wide enough to remove about a fourth of the cabbage. Lift out enough inner leaves to form a shell or bowl about 1-inch thick. Spoon dip into cavity of cabbage and serve with an assortment of fresh vegetables or croutons.

PREP TIME: 1 hour   MAKES: 6 cups

NOTES

_____

_____

_____

_____

_____

_____

POKE SALAD LASAGNA

INGREDIENTS:

1 pound ground beef

1 cup chopped onions

$\frac{1}{2}$ cup chopped celery

$\frac{1}{2}$ cup chopped bell pepper

$\frac{1}{4}$ cup diced garlic

3 cups tomato sauce

1 tsp fresh oregano, chopped

1 tsp fresh basil, chopped

1 tsp fresh thyme, chopped

12 lasagna noodles

2 cups poke salad, cooked and drained (or canned)

1 cup cottage cheese

1 cup ricotta cheese

1 egg, beaten

1 cup Parmesan cheese, grated

1/8 tsp nutmeg

salt and black pepper

METHOD:

Preheat oven to 350 degrees F. In a 12-inch cast iron skillet, saute ground beef until meat is separated grain for grain. Remove beef with a slotted spoon and discard all but 1 teaspoon of the drippings. Add onions, celery, bell pepper and garlic. Saute 3-5 minutes or until vegetables are wilted. Return beef to the skillet and blend into the vegetable mixture. Add tomato puree, oregano, basil and thyme. Season to taste using salt and pepper. Bring mixture to a roiling boil, reduce heat to simmer and cook for 30 minutes. In a two gallon stock pot, cook noodles according to package directions. Drain and set aside. In a medium-size mixing bowl, combine poke salad, cottage cheese, ricotta cheese, egg, parmesan cheese and nutmeg. Using a wooden spoon, mix ingredients thoroughly until well incorporated. Season to taste using salt and pepper. Assemble lasagna by placing 1/3 of the poke salad mixture in the bottom of a lightly greased 9" x 13" pan. Top with 4 noodles and beef mixture. Repeat this process until 3 layers are complete, ending with the beef mixture. Cover pan with aluminum foil and bake 45 minutes until hot and bubbly.

PREP TIME: 1$\frac{1}{2}$ hours   SERVES: 8

NOTES

_____

_____

_____

_____

_____

_____

79

POKE SALAD CORNBREAD

INGREDIENTS:

3 tbsps oil

2 cups yellow corn meal

1/3 cup all purpose flour

1 tbsp sugar

1/2 tsp salt

1 cup chopped poke salad, drained

1/2 cup whole kernel corn, drained

1 3/4 cups milk

1 egg, beaten

METHOD:

Preheat oven to 425 degrees F. Heat oil in a 10-inch cast iron skillet or 9-inch square baking pan in oven for 5 minutes. Remove skillet and tilt to coat bottom evenly. In a large mixing bowl, combine all dry ingredients. Add poke salad, corn, milk and egg. Using a spoon, mix well until all ingredients are well incorporated. Pour into skillet and bake 20-25 minutes until golden brown.

PREP TIME: 45 Minutes   SERVES: 6

LAZY DAY COBBLER

INGREDIENTS:

1 stick butter, melted

1 cup sugar

1 1/2 tsps baking powder

3/4 cup milk

1 cup flour

1/4 tsp salt

1 (20 ounce) can fruit in syrup

1/2 cup sugar

METHOD:

Preheat oven to 350 degrees F. Pour melted butter into the bottom of a 9" x 13" baking pan. Set aside. In a large mixing bowl, place 1 cup of sugar, baking powder, milk, flour and salt. Beat all ingredients well until incorporated. Pour into the bottom of baking pan and do not stir. Top mixture with fruit and remaining sugar. Bake for 45 minutes until batter rises to the top.

PREP TIME: 1 hour   SERVES: 8

NOTES

_____

_____

_____

_____

_____

_____

GATEAU DE FIGUE
(Fig Cake)

INGREDIENTS:

1 pint chopped fresh figs

¾ cup butter

1 cup sugar

3 eggs

2½ cups all purpose flour

1 tsp baking powder

1 tsp baking soda

1 tsp ground nutmeg

1 tsp ground cinnamon

1 tsp ground ginger

1 cup buttermilk

1 tsp vanilla

1 cup chopped pecans

METHOD:

Preheat oven to 350 degrees F. Grease and flour a bundt-style pan and set aside. In a large mixing bowl, cream butter and sugar. Add the eggs, one at a time, blending after each addition. In a separate bowl, combine the flour, baking powder, soda and spices. Add these dry ingredients, alternately with the buttermilk, into the sugar mixture. Stir constantly until all ingredients are well incorporated into the batter. Add vanilla, pecans and figs. Stir well and pour into the greased pan. Bake for approximately 1 hour or until cake tester comes out clean. Allow to cool. Remove from pan. You may wish to serve with ice cream or a dollop of fresh whipped cream.

PREP TIME: 1½ hours   SERVES: 8-10

NOTES

_____

_____

_____

_____

_____

_____

Chapter Five
July

Louisiana Catfish Festival

CATFISH FESTIVAL
Des Allemands, Louisiana

Not satisfied with the title of the "Catfish Capital of the World," a local priest in the small town of Des Allemands, Louisiana set out to the Louisiana Legislature in 1980 to have the town officially proclaimed the "Catfish Capital of the Universe." Father Mac, as he was affectionately known by his parishioners before his death, was the founder of this now-famous festival which is held each year in July as a fundraiser for St. Gertrude Church. Although started small in 1975 as a way to raise money to pay for a leaking church roof, the festival has since attracted national attention and brought recognition to the town's flourishing catfish industry. You will see the festival's religious foundation surface as it opens with a blessing of the food booths by the church priest.

The main food attraction of the festival is, of course, fried catfish. The annual fry grows each year and now takes an amazing 12 to 15 thousand pounds to supply a two-day weekend festival. The fish is all purchased locally from area fishermen and is served on catfish platters, catfish poboys and in that delectable dish, catfish sauce piquante. Festival-goers can also get their fill of other foods such as seafood gumbo, potato salad, soft shell crab poboys, and an array of homemade cakes and candies.

The visitors will never have to worry about boredom at this festival filled with activity. From the Catfish Eating and Cooking Contests to the live music and games, this festival provides a fun-filled weekend for all ages. Look for the Catfish Queen and Junior Catfish Queen on the festival grounds for a warm Des Allemands welcome.

The people of St. Charles Parish and the town of Des Allemands work hard to defend their catfish title by promoting Louisiana Catfish through the Department of Agriculture and by developing the industry for its recreational potential. The towns folk of this small Louisiana town of 3,000 pride themselves on their Catfish Festival celebrating an industry that has put this bayou town "on the map."

Lagniappe

Des Allemands is located midway between the cities of New Orleans to the east and Houma to the west along Highway 90. If you want to travel to the big city, New Orleans has many top attractions such as the French Quarter, Audubon Zoo and Botanical Gardens, and the Aquarium of Americas. Quaint lodging establishments such as the historic Cornstalk Hotel or the Bienville House are good choices. The dining possibilities are endless in this "city that care forgot." Try one or all of the following on your next trip to the "Big Easy": Emeril's, Bayona's, K - Paul's or Uglesich's Restaurant.

If you prefer a drive to the west deep into Bayou Country, travel 30 miles on Highway 90 to Houma and Thibodaux. There you can take a tour of the scenic Louisiana swamps, given in English or French, and listen to great Cajun music on A Cajun Man's Swamp Cruise with Black Guidry. Tour historic plantation homes such as Southdown Museum and drive through the beautiful bayou country that leads down to the Gulf of Mexico.

Travel on I-10 to I-310. Take I-310 to Highway 90 and travel west 11 miles to Des Allemands. The festival is conducted on the grounds of St. Gertrude Church. For more information about the festival, call (504) 566-5068.

Photo: Bill Castel, Heritage Photography
Chef John Folse with Chef Beany McGregor. Clockwise from bottom left: Seafood Stuffed Turban of Catfish, Smoked Catfish & Crawfish Terrine, Catfish Poboy

COUNTRY CATFISH & CORN CHOWDER

INGREDIENTS:

6 (5-7-ounce) catfish fillets, cubed
1 cup whole kernel corn
1 (15.5 ounce) can cream-style corn
1/2 cup melted butter
1 cup diced onions
1 cup diced celery
1/2 cup diced red bell pepper
1/4 cup diced garlic
1 cup flour
3 quarts chicken stock

1 cup heavy whipping cream
1/4 cup sliced green onions
1/4 cup chopped parsley
1 tbsp fresh thyme, chopped
1 tbsp fresh basil, chopped
salt and black pepper
Louisiana Gold Pepper Sauce
1 cup cooked red kidney beans
1 cup cooked lima beans
1 cup grated cheddar cheese

METHOD:

In a 5-quart cast iron dutch oven, heat butter over medium-high heat. Add onions, celery, bell pepper, garlic and 1 cup of whole kernel corn. Saute 3-5 minutes or until vegetables are wilted. Add half of the catfish and blend well into the vegetable mixture, cooking 5-10 minutes longer. Sprinkle in flour and, using a wire whisk, whip until white roux is achieved. Add chicken stock, one ladle at a time, until mixture is smooth and soup-like in consistency. Add heavy whipping cream and cream-style corn. Blend well, bring to a rolling boil and reduce to simmer. Cook 15-20 minutes, stirring occasionally. Additional stock may be added to retain soup-like consistency. Add green onions, parsley, thyme and basil. Season to taste using salt, pepper and Louisiana Gold. Fold in the remaining catfish, kidney and lima beans and cheddar cheese. Stir gently until cheese is melted and fish is perfectly cooked, but not falling apart. Adjust seasonings, if necessary, and serve with hot French bread.

PREP TIME: 1 Hour   SERVES: 6-8

NOTES

_____

_____

_____

_____

_____

SEAFOOD-STUFFED TURBAN OF CATFISH

INGREDIENTS:

6 (5-7 ounce) catfish fillets
2 pounds white or claw crabmeat
³/₄ cup butter
¹/₂ cup chopped onions
¹/₂ cup chopped celery
¹/₂ cup chopped green bell pepper
¹/₂ cup chopped red bell pepper
¹/₄ cup diced garlic

2 cups seasoned Italian bread crumbs
¹/₄ cup chopped parsley
1 tbsp paprika
³/₄ cup water
³/₄ cup white wine
³/₄ cup melted butter
salt and cracked pepper
Louisiana Gold Pepper Sauce

METHOD:

Preheat oven to 375 degrees F. In a 10-inch cast iron skillet, melt ³/₄ cup of butter over medium-high heat. Add onions, celery, bell peppers, and garlic. Saute 3-5 minutes or until vegetables are wilted. Add crabmeat and blend well into vegetable mixture. Continue to cook until juices are rendered from vegetables and crabmeat. Season to taste, using salt and pepper. Remove from heat and sprinkle in bread crumbs, a little at a time, until proper consistency is achieved. Stuffing should not be too dry. Adjust seasonings, if necessary. Place an equal amount of stuffing in each catfish fillet. Roll fillets into turban shape and secure with toothpicks. Place fish in baking pan, then add water, wine and melted butter. Sprinkle with paprika, and season to taste using salt, pepper and Louisiana Gold. Bake for 15 minutes or until golden brown. Garnish with parsley.

PREP TIME: 1 hours   SERVES: 6

NOTES

_____

_____

_____

_____

_____

_____

CATFISH POBOY

INGREDIENTS:

2 (5-7 ounce) catfish fillets
1 quart ice water
2 cups yellow corn meal
salt and black pepper

Louisiana Gold Pepper Sauce
oil for deep frying
French bread

METHOD:

In a home-style Fry Daddy, heat vegetable oil according to manufacturer's directions or to 375 degrees F. Slice the fillets diagonally into 6-7 thin strips. Season the ice water to taste using salt, pepper and Louisiana Gold. Place the catfish in the ice water and allow to sit 10-12 minutes. Many of Louisiana's premier hunting camp cooks swear by the technique of soaking catfish or oysters in seasoned ice water prior to breading and deep frying. The cold temperature keeps the fish moist during cooking and sets the corn meal batter on the outside of the fish. Season corn meal to taste using salt, pepper and Louisiana Gold. Place seasoned corn meal into a paper bag. Remove catfish from water, drain well and toss with the corn meal inside paper bag. Deep fry until fish is golden brown on all sides and floats to the top. Remove, drain and keep warm. Toast poboy-style bread until crispy and dress with your favorite tartar sauce, remoulade, lettuce and tomatoes. Top with hot catfish fillets and serve warm.

PREP TIME: 30 minutes   MAKES: 2-4 poboys

NOTES

_____

_____

_____

_____

_____

_____

LOUISIANA TARTAR SAUCE

INGREDIENTS:

1$\frac{1}{2}$ cups mayonnaise
2 tbsps lemon juice
$\frac{1}{4}$ cup chopped pimento olives
$\frac{1}{4}$ cup chopped sweet pickles
1 tbsp sweet pickle juice

$\frac{1}{4}$ cup chopped parsley
$\frac{1}{4}$ cup chopped capers
1 tbsp sliced green onions
salt and black pepper
Louisiana Gold Pepper Sauce

METHOD:

In a large ceramic bowl, combine mayonnaise and lemon juice. Using a wire whisk, blend until well incorporated. Add olives, pickles, pickle juice, parsley, capers and green onions. Fold all seasoning ingredients into the mayonnaise until mixture is evenly blended. Season to taste using salt, pepper and Louisiana Gold. If you prefer a more tart taste, add a little lemon juice or white vinegar. If a sweeter taste is preferred, add more sweet pickle juice or a touch of sugar. Cover with clear wrap and refrigerate overnight for flavors to develop.

PREP TIME: 15 minutes   MAKES: 2 cups

NOTES

_____

_____

_____

_____

_____

_____

SPANISH-TOWN CATFISH OMELETTE

INGREDIENTS FOR EACH OMELETTE:

$^{1}/_{2}$ cup diced catfish fillets

3 whole eggs

$^{1}/_{4}$ cup melted butter

$^{1}/_{4}$ cup diced onions

$^{1}/_{4}$ cup diced red bell pepper

$^{1}/_{4}$ cup diced tomatoes

1 tsp diced jalapenos

1 tsp chopped garlic

$^{1}/_{4}$ cup V-8 juice

chili powder

$^{1}/_{4}$ cup heavy whipping cream

1 tbsp sliced green onions

1 tbsp chopped parsley

salt and black pepper

Louisiana Gold Pepper Sauce

$^{1}/_{2}$ cup shredded cheddar cheese

METHOD:

In a cast iron chef's pan, heat $^{1}/_{8}$ cup butter over medium-high heat. Add onions, bell pepper, tomatoes, jalapenos and garlic. Saute 3-5 minutes or until vegetables are wilted. Add cubed catfish and blend well into the vegetable mixture. Should mixture become too dry during the cooking process, moisten with V-8 juice. When catfish is cooked, season to taste using chili powder, salt, pepper and Louisiana Gold. Remove and set aside. In a large mixing bowl, combine eggs, heavy whipping cream, green onions and parsley. Using a wire whisk, whip well until blended. Season to taste using salt, pepper and Louisiana Gold. In a separate saute or omelette pan, heat remaining butter over medium-high heat. Pour in egg mixture and cook until omelette begins to set. Spoon the catfish mixture and cheese over one half of the omelette. Fold other half over to cover the filling mixture and continue to cook until omelette is done.

PREP TIME: 30 minutes   SERVES: 1

NOTES

_____

_____

_____

_____

_____

_____

SMOKED CATFISH & CRAWFISH TERRINE

INGREDIENTS:

4 (5-7 ounce) catfish fillets, smoked
1 cup cooked crawfish tails
1 cup mayonnaise
$^1/_2$ cup sour cream
1 tbsp diced garlic
$^1/_4$ cup diced red bell pepper
$^1/_4$ cup diced yellow bell pepper

1 tbsp lemon juice
$^1/_2$ ounce sherry
1 tbsp Worcestershire sauce
salt and black pepper
Louisiana Gold Pepper Sauce
2 pkgs unflavored gelatin,
    dissolved in $^1/_4$ cup of cold water

Note: You may substitute shrimp, lobster or crab for the catfish.

METHOD:

Coarsely chop smoked catfish and crawfish and place in a 2-quart mixing bowl. Add all remaining ingredients, blending well to incorporate seasonings into the mixture. Adjust salt and pepper if necessary, and pour mixture into a terrine mold. Place in refrigerator, covered, overnight. When serving, remove from mold and garnish with French bread or garlic croutons. To enhance the presentation of the terrine, you may wish to color two cups of mayonnaise, one with red food coloring and one with green. Using a pastry bag with a star tip, pipe colored mayonnaise around the base of the terrine. You may also wish to garnish the top of the terrine with a small amount of the colored mayonnaise and a fresh tomato rose.

PREP TIME: 45 minutes   SERVES: 20

NOTES

_____

_____

_____

_____

_____

_____

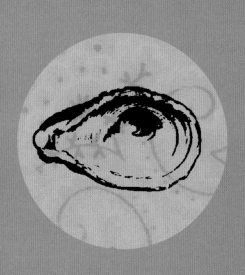

Chapter Six
August

Gueydan Duck Festival

GUEYDAN DUCK FESTIVAL
Gueydan, Louisiana

Visit the Cajun village of Gueydan during the last weekend in August and you will find a festival which celebrates the migratory game bird which is so important to the culture and foods of Louisiana. The Duck is the reason for this celebration which is appropriately held in the "Duck Capital of America." Long noted for its excellent duck and goose hunting during the winter months, Gueydan created this festival in the late 1970s to bring the duck to the forefront and celebrate its significant ties to the local culture. The events and the food all center around the honored bird. A Duck and Goose calling contest tests the quality and accuracy of calls from the young and old alike. Since retrieving is a vital part of hunting, the dog trials feature the best, most highly-trained retrievers who vie for the title. Of course, shooting accuracy is critical to a successful hunt, so the skeet shooting competition is always a very popular contest.

Indoor and outdoor cooking contests turn up some of the best recipes around for preparing wild game. Pot roasted teal has been a festival winner with other entries including Goose and Shrimp Jambalaya and Seafood Sauce Piquante. Of special interest is the fascinating and unique cooking implements used in the outdoor cooking contest.

Be sure to seek out the duck decoy carvers who are happy to put on a demonstration of this intricate and delicate skill. They proudly display the finished products which are impressive to say the least. You will find great music and activities at this festival deep in Cajun country. The small village of 2,500 residents comes alive each August with a celebration of culture and customs that surely warrants a travel south.

Lagniappe

Gueydan, Louisiana is nestled among some of Acadiana's greatest cities. Within a 30 to 60 mile radius, you can travel to Abbeville, Jennings, Crowley, Lafayette and Lake Charles. Bed-and-breakfast lodging and great restaurants are located in these surrounding towns and cites. One example is the Creole Rose Manor in nearby Jennings. The time of the year for the festival is also a great time to go boating, swimming or fishing at Lake Arthur situated near Gueydan. Visit again in the winter months for great duck and goose hunting or sightseeing trips. You may also want to get an informative, information-packed tour of Ellis Stansel's Gourmet Rice Farm where the world famous rice was developed and processed.

Exit I-10 at Estherwood, travel to Highway 90 and take a right, follow Highway 90 to Midland and take Highway 91 south to Gueydan. For more information about the festival, call festival organizers at (318) 235-6263.

Photo: Bill Castel, Heritage Photography
Chef John Folse and Greg Guirard with Pot-Roasted Teal Ducks.

POT-ROASTED TEAL DUCKS

INGREDIENTS:

6 teal ducks
1/2 cup minced garlic
1/2 cup minced green onions
2 tbsps salt
2 tbsps black pepper
1 tsp cayenne pepper
2 bottles Pinot Noir wine
1/2 cup vegetable oil

2 cups diced onions
1 cup diced celery
1 cup diced bell pepper
1/4 cup diced garlic
1 tbsp fresh basil, chopped
1 tsp fresh thyme, chopped
Louisiana Gold Pepper Sauce

METHOD:

Make sure teals are well cleaned inside and out and all visible pin feathers removed from the wings and backs. Drain well and place ducks, breast side down, on a cutting board. Using a paring knife, cut two slits into the breasts from the back following the breast bone, to create two seasoning pouches on each breast. In a small mixing bowl combine, garlic, green onions, salt and peppers. Blend well to create a seasoning mixture. Stuff an equal portion of the seasonings into the slits of each duck breast. Season the ducks inside and out with any of the mixture remaining in the bowl. Place the ducks in a deep bowl and top with Pinot Noir. Cover and place in the refrigerator for 24 hours. In a 7-quart cast iron dutch oven, heat oil over medium-high heat. Drain ducks well and reserve marinade. Season ducks to taste with salt, pepper and Louisiana Gold. Brown the ducks well by turning often until they are golden brown on all sides. Remove and keep warm. Using the same oil, add onions, celery, bell pepper and garlic. Saute 3-5 minutes or until vegetables are wilted. Return ducks to the pot and add red wine marinade. NOTE: A small amount of chicken stock may be added as the ducks cook to retain volume and increase flavor. Bring the wine to a rolling boil, reduce to simmer, cover, and cook until ducks are tender, approximately 1 1/2-2 hours. Serve over dirty rice.

PREP TIME: 3 hours   SERVES: 6

NOTES

_____

_____

_____

_____

_____

_____

DUCK, ANDOUILLE & OYSTER GUMBO

INGREDIENTS:

2 mallard ducks, cut into serving pieces
$^1/_2$ pound sliced andouille
2 pints select oysters
1 cup vegetable oil
1$^1/_2$ cups flour
2 cups chopped onions
1 cup chopped celery
1 cup chopped bell pepper

$^1/_4$ cup diced garlic
3 quarts chicken stock
12 chicken livers
2 cups sliced green onions
1 cup chopped parsley
salt and black pepper
Louisiana Gold Pepper Sauce

METHOD:

In a 2-gallon stock pot, heat oil over medium-high heat. Once oil is hot, add flour and, using a wire whisk, stir until roux is golden brown. Do not scorch. Should black specks appear, discard and begin again. Add onions, celery, bell pepper and garlic. Saute 3-5 minutes or until vegetables are wilted. Add duck and andouille and saute in roux approximately 15 minutes. Add chicken stock, one ladle at a time, stirring constantly until all is incorporated. Bring to a rolling boil, reduce to simmer and add chicken livers and oysters. Cook 1 hour or until duck is tender, adding stock as needed to retain volume of liquid. Add green onions and parsley. Season to taste using salt, pepper and Louisiana Gold. Cook an additional 5 minutes and serve over cooked rice.

PREP TIME: 1$^1/_2$ hours   SERVES: 12

NOTES

_____

_____

_____

_____

_____

_____

CAJUN DUCK FAJITAS

INGREDIENTS:

3 duck breasts

¹/₄ cup vegetable oil

¹/₂ cup sliced onions

¹/₂ cup julienned green bell pepper

¹/₂ cup julienned red bell pepper

1 tbsp chopped garlic

1 cup shredded lettuce

1 cup diced tomatoes

1 cup prepared guacamole

1 bag tortilla shells

salt and black pepper

cumin

chili powder

Louisiana Gold Pepper Sauce

METHOD:

In a 3-quart cast iron dutch oven, place ducks in lightly salted water. Bring to a rolling boil, reduce to simmer and cook until tender. Drain and debone meat, cutting into ¹/₂-inch strips. In a 10-inch cast iron skillet, heat oil over medium-high heat. Season duck with salt, pepper, cumin, chili powder and Louisiana Gold. Stir-fry the duck breasts in the hot oil until golden brown. Add onions, bell peppers and garlic. Reduce heat to medium, cover, and allow vegetables to wilt over the sizzling duck. In a separate cast iron skillet, heat tortilla shells until thoroughly warm. Assemble fajitas by spreading guacamole over the hot tortillas, adding small amounts of the lettuce and tomatoes, and topping each with an equal amount of the duck, onions and peppers. Roll, jelly-roll fashion, and heat until warm.

PREP TIME: 1¹/₂ hours   SERVES: 6

NOTES

_____

_____

_____

_____

_____

_____

SMOKED DUCK HAM

INGREDIENTS:

4 mallard duck breasts

2 tsps salt

1 tsp black pepper

1 tbsp diced garlic

1 tbsp fresh thyme, chopped

1 tbsp fresh basil, chopped

1 tbsp fresh tarragon, chopped

½ cup dry red wine

¼ cup Steen's cane syrup or maple syrup

2 tbsps vegetable oil

2 bottles root beer

METHOD:

In a large mixing bowl, combine duck breasts with all remaining ingredients, except root beer. Massage the seasonings well into the breasts. Pour all ingredients from the bowl into a Ziploc bag. Place in the refrigerator for 2 days prior to smoking. Turn the bag often over the 2 days. Heat a home-style smoker according to manufacture's directions. Into the water pan, place one quart of water and the root beer. Soak your favorite wood chips in water and, when ready to cook, place the duck breasts on the top of the smoker. Pour remaining marinating liquid into the water pan of the smoker. Throw two generous handfuls of wet smoke wood onto the hot coals and allow the breasts to smoke for approximately 1 hour or until done to your liking. Once done, slice each breast into 6-8 slices and serve with your favorite dipping sauce or as an entree.

PREP TIME: 2 hours   SERVES: 6

NOTES

_____

_____

_____

_____

_____

_____

CREOLE DIRTY RICE

INGREDIENTS:

1/2 pound chicken gizzards
1/2 pound chicken livers
1/2 cup melted butter
1 cup diced onions
1 cup diced celery
1 cup diced bell pepper
2 tbsps diced garlic

1 cup chicken stock
6 cups cooked rice
1/2 cup sliced green onions
1/2 cup chopped parsley
salt and black pepper
Louisiana Gold Pepper Sauce

METHOD:

In a small sauce pot, poach chicken gizzards in lightly salted water until tender, approximately 45 minutes. Remove, cool and reserve poaching liquid. Using a sharp paring knife, remove all tough membrane, and chop the gizzards into tiny pieces. Set aside. In a 3- quart cast iron dutch oven, heat butter over medium-high heat. Saute chicken livers until golden brown on all sides, approximately 15-20 minutes. Remove chicken livers from saute pan and place on a chopping board to cool. Into the same dutch oven, add onions, celery, bell pepper and garlic. Saute 3-5 minutes or until vegetables are wilted. Once vegetables are done, coarsely chop chicken livers and return with gizzards to the dutch oven. Add chicken stock and a small amount of the poaching liquid, bring to a low boil and cook until volume of liquid is reduced to approximately 1/4 cup. Add cooked white rice, blending well into the meat mixture, and garnish using green onions and parsley. Season to taste using salt, pepper and Louisiana Gold.

PREP TIME: 1 hour   SERVES: 6-8

NOTES

_____

_____

_____

_____

_____

_____

Chapter Seven
September

Festivals Acadiens
Frog Festival
Louisiana Shrimp & Petroleum Festival
Louisiana Sugarcane Festival
Madisonville Wooden Boat Festival

FESTIVALS ACADIENS
Lafayette, Louisiana

Visitors to the Acadian City of Lafayette can enjoy four festivals simultaneously as they celebrate the rhythm of Cajun life at Festivals Acadiens. During the third weekend each September, the city comes alive and pays tribute to the Cajun culture with a combination of festivals including the Festival de Musique Acadienne, the Bayou Food Festival, the Louisiana Native Crafts Festival, and Downtown Alive! and Kids Alive! This great combination of gatherings features the best in Cajun and Zydeco music, Cajun and Creole food and native Louisiana crafts.

The events that comprise Festivals Acadiens joined forces in 1977 to celebrate and preserve the Cajun culture. Each festival has a unique history and now, together, they draw over 100,000 visitors to the city each year.

The 23-year old Louisiana Native Crafts Festival is the oldest event of Festivals Acadiens. It features over 300 traditional and contemporary craftspersons, cooks, storytellers, dancers, singers and artisans. See what times were like when activities and pastimes such as folk dancing, alligator skinning, storytelling and boat building were a part of everyday life.

Festival de Musique Acadienne, originally the Tribute to Cajun Music Festival, now features Louisiana's best Cajun and Zydeco bands and draws people from the United States, Canada, France and Europe.

After working up an appetite with all of this activity, stroll over to the Bayou Food Festival where you will find one of the largest arrays of Cajun and Creole dishes of any Louisiana festival. Try the alligator sauce piquante, seafood jambalaya, chicken and sausage gumbo, boudin, crawfish pie or succulent shrimp on a stick.

Finally, Downtown Alive! is Lafayette's premier TGIF party featuring a Friday night concert in the streets of downtown. The noon concert and activities are now dedicated to kids and called Kids Alive!

There is also plenty of Lagniappe, or extra, as the neighboring towns celebrate the festival weekend with activities of their own. Travel to this hub of Cajun life to celebrate a culture and a people like no other. The Festivals Acadiens offers great festivity with French Louisiana flair.

Lagniappe

A visit to Lafayette is sure to be one filled with activity. Top sites to see in the city are the Acadian Village, Vermilionville and the Acadian Cultural Center Jean Lafitte National Park, which all provide visitors a glimpse into the rich history of the Cajun life. You should stay at one of the historic bed-and-breakfasts located either in the city or in one of the picturesque Cajun towns that border Lafayette. There is Belle of the Oaks in nearby Carencro or La Grande Maison in Broussard. A drive through the small, scenic towns that surround the city is a great way to spend extra days before or after the festival. Breaux Bridge, Broussard, New Iberia, Mamou, Eunice, Opelousas, Washington and St. Martinville are all examples of towns where you will find great examples of Cajun life. When you are looking for a place to enjoy some great Cajun food try Randal's Restaurant and Cajun Dancehall, Enola Prudhomme's, Prejean's or Mulate's in Breaux Bridge.

Travel to Lafayette via I-10, I-49 or Highway 90. Admission to most festival events is free. For more information about the festivals which comprise Festivals Acadiens, call the Lafayette Convention and Visitors Commission at (318) 232-3808 or (800) 346-1958 or (800) 543-5340 in Canada.

Photo: Bill Castel, Heritage Photography
Chef John Folse and Michael Doucet of BeauSoleil with a platter of speckled trout and fresh crawfish tails.

HOG'S HEAD CHEESE

INGREDIENTS FOR STOCK:

1 hog head, split and cleaned
4 pig's feet, scraped and cleaned
4 pounds pork butt
3 cups finely diced onions
3 cups finely diced celery
2 cups finely diced bell pepper
$\frac{1}{2}$ cup finely diced garlic
2 whole bay leaves
1 tsp dry thyme

$\frac{1}{4}$ cup whole peppercorns
$\frac{1}{2}$ cup finely sliced green onions
$\frac{1}{2}$ cup finely diced parsley
$\frac{1}{2}$ cup finely diced red bell pepper
$\frac{1}{2}$ cup finely diced carrots
salt and cracked black pepper
3 envelopes unflavored gelatin,
dissolved in $\frac{1}{2}$ cup water

METHOD:

In a 4-gallon stock pot, place all of the above ingredients up to and including the whole peppercorns. Add enough water to cover the contents by three inches and bring to a rolling boil. Using a ladle, skim all foam and other impurities that rise to the surface during the first $\frac{1}{2}$ hour of boiling. Continue to cook until meat is tender and pulling away from the bones, approximately $2\frac{1}{2}$ hours. Remove all meat from stock pot and lay out on a flat baking pan to cool. Strain and reserve 10 cups of the cooking stock and discard vegetables. Return stock to a low boil. Add all remaining ingredients, except gelatin and salt and pepper. Boil for 3 minutes and remove from heat. Season to taste using salt and pepper. Add dissolved gelatin and set aside. Once meat has cooled, remove all bones and finely chop in a food processor. Place equal amounts of the meat in four trays and ladle in hot seasoned stock. The mixture should be meaty with just enough stock to gel and hold the meat together. Cover with clear wrap and place in refrigerator to set overnight. Head cheese is best eaten as an appetizer with croutons or crackers.

PREP TIME: 3 hours   MAKES: 4 one-pound trays

NOTES

_____

_____

_____

_____

_____

_____

Senator Ellender's Oyster Jambalaya

INGREDIENTS:

3 pints oysters
5 tbsps vegetable oil
1 tbsp flour
2 cups diced onions
1 cup diced celery
$\frac{1}{2}$ cup diced bell pepper
$\frac{1}{4}$ cup diced garlic
1 cup tomato sauce
1 lemon, chopped
1 lemon rind, grated

2 bay leaves
Worcestershire Sauce
$\frac{1}{2}$ tsp fresh thyme
$\frac{1}{2}$ tsp fresh basil
$\frac{1}{4}$ cup sliced green onions
$\frac{1}{4}$ cup chopped parsley
salt and black pepper
Louisiana Gold Pepper Sauce
3 cups raw rice
$4\frac{1}{2}$ cups water

METHOD:

In a 5-quart cast iron dutch oven, heat oil over medium-high heat. Add flour and, using a wire whisk, whip until light brown roux is achieved. Add onions, celery, bell pepper and garlic. Saute 3-5 minutes or until vegetables are wilted. Add tomato sauce, lemon, lemon rind, bay leaves, Worcestershire, thyme and basil. Continue to saute an additional 5 minutes until all ingredients are incorporated. Season to taste using salt, pepper and Louisiana Gold. Allow sauce to simmer for approximately 30 minutes. Add oysters, bring to a rolling boil and simmer for an additional 5 minutes. Add green onions and parsley, stirring well into the tomato sauce mixture. Add rice and water. Adjust seasonings to taste using salt, pepper and Louisiana Gold. Bring mixture to a boil, cover, reduce to simmer and allow to cook for 30 minutes. *NOTE: Do not lift the lid or stir the jambalaya.* Serve hot with a slice of French bread.

PREP TIME: $1\frac{1}{2}$ hours   SERVES: 6

NOTES

_____
_____
_____
_____
_____

TROUT CYPREMORT

INGREDIENTS:

8 speckled trout fillets

$^1/_4$ cup butter

$^1/_4$ cup flour

1 cup chopped onions

$^1/_2$ cup chopped celery

$^1/_2$ cup chopped bell pepper

$^1/_4$ cup diced garlic

1 cup sliced mushrooms

$^1/_4$ cup white wine

1 tbsp lemon pepper

1 pound lump crabmeat

2 cups fish stock

$^1/_2$ cup whipping cream

salt and black pepper

Louisiana Gold Pepper Sauce

1 cup seasoned flour

$^1/_2$ cup vegetable oil

METHOD:

Preheat oven to 350 degrees F. In a 10-inch cast iron skillet, melt butter over medium-high heat. Add flour and, using a wire whisk, whip constantly until light brown roux is achieved. Add onions, celery, bell pepper, garlic and mushrooms. Saute 3-5 minutes or until vegetables are wilted. Add wine, lemon pepper and crabmeat, blending well into the vegetable mixture. Add stock, one ladle at a time, and cream, stirring until all is incorporated. Season to taste using salt, pepper and Louisiana Gold. Remove from heat and keep warm. In a separate 10-inch cast iron skillet, heat oil over medium-high heat. Season flour using salt, pepper and Louisiana Gold. Dredge fillets in flour and pan fry until golden brown on all sides. Place on drain pan and then onto cookie sheet. Ladle crab sauce on top of each fillet and bake for approximately 20 minutes.

PREP TIME: 1 hour   SERVES: 6

NOTES

_____

_____

_____

_____

_____

LEMON BUTTER QUAIL

INGREDIENTS:

8 quail

$^1/_2$ cup butter

4 tbsps lemon juice

$^1/_2$ lemon peel, minced

$^1/_4$ cup diced garlic

$^1/_4$ cup sliced green onions

8 slices bacon

$^1/_4$ cup chopped parsley

salt and black pepper

Louisiana Gold Pepper Sauce

METHOD:

Preheat oven to 350 degrees F. In a 10-inch cast iron skillet, melt butter over medium high heat. Add lemon juice, peel, garlic and green onions. Saute 3-5 minutes or until vegetables are wilted. Wrap bacon strip around each quail breast and hold in place with a toothpick. Place quail, breast side up, in a 9" x 12" baking pan and drape with foil. Thoroughly baste each bird with butter sauce. Bake for 20 minutes, basting occasionally, to prevent birds from drying out. After 20 minutes, remove foil, turn birds breast side down and brown 10 additional minutes. Remove birds and keep warm. For gravy, dissolve 1 teaspoon of corn starch in $^1/_2$ cup warm water and add to drippings in baking dish. Stir over low heat, reduce to $^1/_2$ volume and adjust seasonings if necessary. Return birds to baking dish and baste with gravy prior to serving. Garnish with parsley.

PREP TIME: 2 hours   SERVES: 4

NOTES

_____

_____

_____

_____

_____

_____

HOT CRAWFISH SPINACH SALAD

INGREDIENTS:

6 ounces crawfish tails
1 (12-ounce) bunch fresh spinach
$^1/_2$ cup vegetable oil
1 cup chopped onions
$^1/_2$ cup chopped celery
$^1/_2$ cup chopped yellow bell pepper
$^1/_4$ cup diced garlic
$^1/_4$ cup Creole mustard

$^1/_4$ cup Steen's cane syrup vinegar
1 tbsp Steen's cane syrup
$^1/_2$ cup diced tomatoes
$^1/_2$ lemon, sliced
$^1/_2$ cup sliced mushrooms
salt and black pepper
Louisiana Gold Pepper Sauce

METHOD:

In 10-inch cast iron skillet, heat oil over medium-high heat. Add onions, celery, bell pepper and garlic. Saute 3-5 minutes or until vegetables are wilted. Whisk in mustard, vinegar, cane syrup and season to taste using salt, pepper and Louisiana Gold. Fold in crawfish and cook until thoroughly heated. Break spinach into bite-size pieces and place in the center of a ceramic bowl. Pour crawfish dressing over spinach and toss to coat well. Garnish with tomato, lemon and mushrooms.

PREP TIME: 30 minutes   SERVES: 4

NOTES

_____

_____

_____

_____

_____

_____

FROG FESTIVAL
Rayne, Louisiana

Hopping with festivity, the annual Rayne Frog Festival welcomes visitors to this great southwest Louisiana town each September. Official ambassador of the "Frog Capital of the World," M'sieur Jacques, the friendly frog, will welcome everyone to this celebration where frogs take center stage. Guests of the festival will revel in the shows featuring these stars. They include the frog racing and jumping contests, Frog Festival Queen competition, frog parade, frog cooking contest, and yes, frog eating contest in which contestants are judged on speed and table manners.

At the Arts and Crafts area, you will find any item imaginable featuring this festival's namesake. Frog earrings, frog doorstops, frog posters and so much more.

The town prides itself on cleanliness and catering to its growing tourist population. Town pride is evident as you experience not only this feature festival, but the many other attractions of the area as Rayne continues to prove the ideal backdrop for such festivities. You'll be welcomed to the town by a colorful row of banners atop light poles called the "Boulevard of Banners" which are among its many claims to fame. Rayne also boasts a listing in *Ripley's Believe It or Not!* as the only town in the country with a known cemetery facing north AND south.

So, go "frog-wild" at the Frog Festival in Rayne, Louisiana. It's just a leap down the Interstate from Lafayette and Lake Charles.

Lagniappe

Rayne is located along Interstate 10 in southwest Louisiana just a few miles west of the city of Lafayette. While in town for the festival, try a stay at either of the quaint bed-and-breakfast establishments, Maison DaBoval or Maison D'Memoire. For activities in Rayne, take a tour of the cities famous murals. Known as the "Louisiana City of Murals," Rayne has many of its downtown buildings painted with colorful murals of frogs and other elements representing the local culture. Louisiana Avenue is filled with shopping opportunities, antique malls and historical sites. A meal at the local Warehouse Restaurant is a sure winner.

For travel outside Rayne, the Acadian city of Lafayette, where tourist attractions and dining options are plentiful, along with the Cajun communities surrounding it, are your best bet. Travel on I-10 to the Rayne/Church Point Exit, go right on Oak Street, then right on Gossen Memorial Drive to the festival grounds. For more information about the festival, call the Rayne Chamber of Commerce & Agriculture at (318) 334- 2332.

Photo: Bill Castel, Heritage Photography
Chef John Folse and Martha Royer. Clockwise from bottom left: Osso Bucco of Frog Legs, Frog Legs Fettuccini, Crabmeat Stuffed Frog Legs, Crackling Biscuits.

OSSO BUCCO OF FROG LEGS

INGREDIENTS:

18 frog legs, cleaned
$^1/_2$ cup olive oil
$^1/_2$ cup flour
1 tbsp fresh thyme, chopped
1 tbsp fresh basil, chopped
$^1/_2$ cup diced carrots
$^1/_2$ cup diced potatoes
$^1/_2$ cup diced zucchini
$^1/_2$ cup diced squash
10 pearl onions
$^1/_2$ cup diced onions

$^1/_2$ cup diced celery
$^1/_2$ cup diced red bell pepper
$^1/_4$ cup diced garlic
1 quart beef stock
$^1/_2$ cup red wine
$^1/_2$ cup sliced green onions
$^1/_4$ cup chopped parsley
salt and black pepper
dash of Worcestershire Sauce
Louisiana Gold Pepper Sauce

METHOD:

In a 10-inch cast iron skillet, heat olive oil over medium-high heat. Season flour to taste using thyme, basil, salt, pepper and Louisiana Gold. Dredge frog legs in flour, shaking off excess. Place in olive oil and sear until lightly browned on each side. Do not overcook. Add carrots, potatoes, zucchini, squash, onions, celery, bell pepper and garlic. Saute 3-5 minutes or until vegetables are wilted. Add beef stock, one ladle at a time, until well blended. Add red wine and stir into mixture. Season to taste using salt, pepper, Worcestershire and Louisiana Gold. Cover pot and cook for 30 minutes or until tender. Add green onions and parsley and serve with pasta or rice.

PREP TIME: 1$^1/_2$ hours   SERVES: 6

NOTES

_____

_____

_____

_____

_____

CRABMEAT-STUFFED FROG LEGS

INGREDIENTS:

18 frog legs, cleaned and deboned
1 pound claw crabmeat
¼ cup minced onions
¼ cup minced celery
¼ cup minced red bell pepper
¼ cup minced yellow bell pepper
¼ cup minced garlic
½ cup mayonnaise
½ cup Creole mustard
1 tbsp fresh thyme, chopped
1 tbsp fresh basil, chopped
½ cup seasoned Italian bread crumbs
1 cup vegetable oil

1 cup chopped onions
1 cup chopped celery
1 cup chopped bell pepper
¼ cup diced garlic
1 cup chopped tomatoes
½ cup sliced black olives
1 cup tomato sauce
2 cups chicken stock
½ cup sliced green onions
¼ cup chopped parsley
salt and black pepper
Louisiana Gold Pepper Sauce

METHOD:

In a large mixing bowl, place crabmeat, onions, celery, bell peppers, garlic, mayonnaise and mustard. Stir well until fully incorporated. Season to taste using thyme, basil, salt and pepper. Sprinkle in bread crumbs and mix until well blended. Stuff frog legs with equal portions of the dressing. Secure opening with a toothpick. Set aside. In a 14-inch cast iron skillet, heat oil over medium-high heat. Add frog legs and season to taste using salt, pepper and Louisiana Gold. Fry until legs are golden brown on all sides. Add remaining onions, celery, bell pepper and garlic. Saute 3-5 minutes or until vegetables are wilted. Add tomatoes, olives and tomato sauce. Mix all ingredients until well blended. Pour in chicken stock and stir until all is incorporated. Bring to a rolling boil, reduce to simmer and cook 20-30 minutes. Prior to serving, add green onions and parsley. Serve with pasta or egg noodles.

PREP TIME: 1 hour   SERVES: 6

NOTES

113

FROG LEGS FETTUCCINI

INGREDIENTS:

12 frog legs

1¹/₂ cups milk

¹/₂ cup butter

1 cup chopped onions

¹/₂ cup chopped celery

¹/₂ cup chopped bell pepper

¹/₄ cup diced garlic

2 tbsps flour

¹/₂ cup diced pimentos

2 cups half-and-half

1 tbsp jalapeno peppers

¹/₄ cup sliced green onions

¹/₄ cup chopped parsley

salt and black pepper

Louisiana Gold Pepper Sauce

¹/₂ pound Velveeta cheese, sliced 1/2-inch thick

¹/₄ cup Parmesan cheese

1 package fettuccini noodles

METHOD:

Snip off tailbone at top of frog legs and cut apart. Wash legs in ice water and soak in 1¹/₂ cups milk for 1 hour in refrigerator. Pat dry with paper towel and season to taste using salt and pepper. Preheat oven to 350 degrees F. In a 10-inch cast iron skillet, melt butter over medium-high heat. Add onions, celery, bell pepper and garlic. Saute 3-5 minutes or until vegetables are wilted. Sprinkle in flour and blend well into the vegetable mixture. Add pimentos, cream and jalapenos, stirring constantly to incorporate all ingredients. Add frog legs, green onions and parsley. Season to taste using salt, pepper and Louisiana Gold. Cook, covered, on low heat approximately 20 minutes, stirring occasionally. Additional cream may be needed to retain consistency. In a 4-quart stock pot, cook fettuccini according to package directions. Drain and place into a 3-quart casserole dish. Add Velveeta cheese and blend thoroughly. Pour the cooked sauce over the fettuccini, top with Parmesan cheese and bake until bubbly.

PREP TIME: 1 hour   SERVES: 6

NOTES

_____

_____

_____

_____

_____

BAKED FROG LEGS

INGREDIENTS:

18 frog legs, cleaned

$^1/_4$ cup melted butter

$^1/_2$ lemon, sliced

1 cup minced onions

$^1/_2$ cup minced bell pepper

$^1/_4$ cup minced garlic

$^1/_2$ cup bottled Italian dressing

$^1/_4$ cup chopped parsley

salt and black pepper

Louisiana Gold Pepper Sauce

paprika for color

METHOD:

Preheat oven to 425 degrees F. In a large ceramic bowl, combine all ingredients, except frog legs. Place frog legs in a 9" x 12" baking dish. Top with sauce and marinate for approximately 1 hour. Bake for approximately 30 minutes, stirring every few minutes. Garnish with paprika, additional lemon slices and parsley. Serve with French bread.

PREP TIME: 1$^1/_2$ hours   SERVES: 6

_____

_____

_____

_____

_____

_____

CRACKLIN' BISCUITS

INGREDIENTS:

4 cups all-purpose flour

2 tbsps baking powder

1 tsp baking soda

1$\frac{1}{2}$ tbsps sugar

1 tsp salt

$\frac{2}{3}$ cup unsalted butter

1$\frac{1}{2}$ cups buttermilk

$\frac{3}{4}$ cup chopped hog cracklin's

$\frac{1}{4}$ cup melted butter

METHOD:

Preheat oven to 400 degrees F. In a large mixing bowl, combine flour, baking powder, baking soda, sugar and salt. Mix well to ensure proper blending. Using a pastry blender, cut $\frac{2}{3}$ cup of butter into flour mixture. Once butter has been well blended into flour, add buttermilk and chopped cracklin's. Continue to mix until biscuit dough is well formed. Place dough on a floured board and knead lightly. Roll dough out until approximately 1-inch thick. Cut biscuits with a 3-inch biscuit cutter until all are formed. Place biscuits in a greased 12-inch cast iron skillet and drizzle with remaining melted butter. Bake until golden brown, approximately 25 minutes.

PREP TIME: 30 minutes   MAKES: 8-10 biscuits

NOTES

_____

_____

_____

_____

_____

_____

LOUISIANA SHRIMP & PETROLEUM FESTIVAL
Morgan City, Louisiana

Each Labor Day weekend, an extravaganza takes place in Morgan City, Louisiana to showcase two of the state's most important natural resources — seafood and oil. For over 60 years, the tri-cities of Berwick, Patterson and Morgan City have honored the working men and women of this area at this gala celebration rated in the top 20 events by the Louisiana Office of Tourism.

Although once known as the Louisiana Shrimp Festival, the festival name was changed in 1967 to pay tribute to the offshore oil and gas production which rapidly revolutionized the local economy after its discovery in 1947.

Deep in Bayou Country in the Atchafalaya Basin near the Gulf of Mexico, Morgan City proves to be the ideal location for this festival which *Time* magazine once described as one of "the best, the most unusual, the most down-home, the most moving and the most fun that the Country has to offer."

Most of the festivities are conducted in the Downtown Historic District and continue for five days. The city comes alive with culinary delights, live music and fascinating events such as the now-famous Blessing of the Fleet. This not-to-be-missed event features elaborately decorated shrimp trawlers, pleasure craft and some of the biggest boats from the oil patch as they are ceremoniously blessed with holy water by a local priest. The boats can be seen circling the river while the King's and Queen's boat meet in a bow-to-bow "kiss" for the traditional champagne toast.

The Children's Village is a fantasyland for kids featuring an enchanted forest, fire-breathing dragon, mysterious castle, storytellers and more.

At this festival, you can relax under the majestic oaks and enjoy the "Music in the Park" celebration where you will hear traditional Cajun, swamp rock, zydeco, country and rhythm and blues. You will experience culinary treasures at the Cajun Culinary Classic. Other attractions include a spectacular fireworks display, a street parade, square dancing, an arts and crafts/antique show and sale, and a rodeo and fishing tournament.

Join the thousands who flock to bayou country each Labor Day weekend and herald this festival as one of the best.

Lagniappe

Morgan City, Louisiana is in the Cajun heartland and has long been synonymous with seafood; the best known — its jumbo shrimp. It is also a hub of Louisiana's oil industry as is evident by the many related businesses which line the highways. Some of the lodging choices in the immediate area include the Holiday Inn, Acadian Inn and Forest Best Western. While in the city, popular restaurant choices are Landry's Seafood, Scully's and The Harbor Restaurant. For Creole cuisine, try The Forest Restaurant in nearby Franklin. A drive to the northwest on Highway 90 will take you through the Cajun towns of Franklin, Jeanerette and New Iberia which lead to the city of Lafayette. A 30-mile drive to the east will take you to the picturesque city of Thibodaux, home of Nicholls State University, where you can tour working sugar mills, plantation homes and numerous historic churches.

Travel to Morgan City via Highway 90 or 70. The majority of festival activities are conducted in the Downtown Historic District. For more information, call the Louisiana Shrimp & Petroleum Festival & Fair Association at (800) 256-2931 or (504) 385-0703.

Photo: Bill Castel, Heritage Photography
Chef John Folse and Mark Defelice. Clockwise from bottom left: Jumbo Shrimp Viala, a platter of shrimp, BBQ Shrimp, Mardi Gras Pasta and Boiled Shrimp.

BBQ SHRIMP

INGREDIENTS:

24 (21-25 count) shrimp, head-on
1/4 pound butter
1/4 cup chopped garlic
1/4 cup minced purple shallots
1/4 cup sliced green onions
1/4 cup sliced red bell pepper
1 tbsp chopped basil

1 tbsp chopped thyme
1/4 cup Worcestershire Sauce
1 bottle Abita Beer
salt and black pepper
Louisiana Gold Pepper Sauce
1/4 pound cold butter, sliced

METHOD:

In a 14-inch cast iron skillet, melt butter over medium-high heat. Add garlic, shallots, green onions and bell pepper. Saute 3-5 minutes or until vegetables are wilted. Add shrimp, basil, thyme and Worcestershire. Simmer shrimp, turning often, until pink and curled, approximately 3-5 minutes. Add beer, salt, pepper and Louisiana Gold. Cook until all liquids have reduced to 1/2 volume. Add 2-3 pats of cold butter, swirling constantly, to incorporate into the sauce. Continue until all butter is used. Remove from heat. Serve 4 shrimp per person with equal amounts of sauce and hot French bread.

PREP TIME: 30 minutes   SERVES: 6

BOILED SHRIMP

INGREDIENTS:

30 quarts cold water
12 medium onions, quartered
6 heads of garlic, slit in half, exposing pods
1 dozen lemons, quartered
1 quart cooking oil
4 pounds salt

1/2 pound cayenne pepper
4 (3-ounce) bags crab boil
24 medium red potatoes
12 ears of corn
50 pounds cleaned shrimp

METHOD:

In a 60-quart stockpot, bring water to a rolling boil. Add onions, garlic, lemons, cooking oil, salt, pepper and crab boil. Continue to boil for 30 minutes. This boiling of the vegetables will ensure a good flavor in the boiling liquid. Add red potatoes and cook approximately 10-12 minutes. Add corn and cook 10 minutes before adding the shrimp. Once the water returns to a boil, cook shrimp 7-10 minutes, turn off heat and allow to set in boiling liquid 12 additional minutes. Shrimp should be served hot with potatoes, corn and pitchers of ice cold beer.

PREP TIME: 2 hours   SERVES: 12

NOTES

_____

_____

_____

CREOLE RATATOUILLE

INGREDIENTS:

2 cups diced eggplant

2 cups (70-90 count) shrimp, peeled and deveined

2 cups diced zucchini

2 cups diced yellow squash

1 cup diced tomato

¹/₂ cup sliced black olives

¹/₂ cup olive oil

1 pound sliced smoked sausage

1 cup chopped onions

1 cup chopped celery

¹/₄ cup chopped red bell pepper

¹/₄ cup chopped yellow bell pepper

¹/₄ cup diced garlic

2 cups tomato sauce

¹/₄ cup chopped thyme

¹/₄ cup chopped basil

¹/₄ cup fresh oregano

salt and black pepper

Louisiana Gold Pepper Sauce

METHOD:

Preheat oven to 375 degrees F. In a 14-inch cast iron skillet, heat olive oil over medium-high heat. Saute smoked sausage until golden brown. Remove and set aside. Add onions, celery, bell peppers and garlic. Saute 3-5 minutes or until vegetables are wilted. Add eggplant, shrimp, zucchini, squash, tomatoes, black olives and sausage. Saute 30 minutes, stirring occasionally to keep from scorching. Once eggplant mixture is wilted, add tomato sauce, thyme, basil and oregano. Stir into vegetable mixture. Season to taste using salt, pepper and Louisiana Gold. Continue to cook 10-15 minutes. Remove from heat and spoon ratatouille into an oven-proof baking dish. Bake, uncovered, for 30 minutes. Serve as a vegetable casserole or as a stuffing for chicken and game birds.

PREP TIME: 1¹/₂ hours   SERVES: 6-8

NOTES

_____

_____

_____

_____

_____

_____

Jumbo Shrimp Viala

INGREDIENTS:

3 dozen (10-12 count) shrimp, head-on

1 pound jumbo lump crabmeat

$^1/_2$ cup melted butter

$^1/_2$ cup finely diced onions

$^1/_2$ cup finely diced celery

$^1/_4$ cup finely diced red bell pepper

2 tbsps finely diced garlic

$^1/_2$ cup sliced green onions

1 tsp dried thyme

1 tsp dried basil

1 tbsp Creole mustard

1 tbsp dry sherry

$^1/_2$ cup Bechamel Sauce

$^3/_4$ cup seasoned Italian bread crumbs

salt and black pepper

$^1/_2$ cup melted butter

$^1/_2$ cup dry sherry

1 cup water

METHOD:

Preheat oven to 350 degrees F. Place shrimp, right side up, on cutting board. Using a sharp paring knife, cut through the tail shell from the top of the tail to the bottom of the flipper, making sure not to separate head from tail. Using your thumbs, open the tail flat, remove the vein and gently pry the meat away from the shell, leaving it intact at the head. Set aside. In a large mixing bowl, combine all of the above ingredients except crabmeat, salt, pepper and the last three ingredients. Using a large mixing spoon, blend until all ingredients are well incorporated. Gently fold in crabmeat being careful not to break lumps. Season to taste using salt and pepper. Stuff tail of shrimp with generous portion of crabmeat stuffing. Once stuffed, the tail should lay flat on a baking pan. Place stuffed shrimp on a large baking sheet and drizzle with butter and sherry. Pour water into the bottom of the baking pan and place on center oven rack. Bake until stuffing is golden brown, approximately 15 minutes.

PREP TIME: 1 hour   SERVES: 6

NOTES

_____

_____

_____

_____

_____

MARDI GRAS PASTA

INGREDIENTS:

3 cups cooked spinach fettuccine
1/4 pound butter
1 tbsp chopped garlic
1/4 cup chopped green onions
1/4 cup sliced mushrooms
1/2 cup diced tomatoes
1/2 cup diced andouille
1/2 cup (50 count) shrimp, peeled and deveined

1/2 cup cooked crawfish tails
1 ounce dry white wine
1 tbsp lemon juice
1 cup heavy whipping cream
1/4 cup diced red bell pepper
1/4 pound chipped cold butter
1 tbsp chopped parsley
salt and cracked pepper

METHOD:

In a 3-quart cast iron sauce pan, melt butter over medium-high heat. Add garlic, green onions, mushrooms, tomatoes and andouille. Saute 3-5 minutes or until all vegetables are wilted. Add shrimp and crawfish. Cook for an additional 2 minutes. Deglaze pan with white wine and lemon juice, and continue cooking until volume of liquid is reduced to half. Add heavy whipping cream and, stirring constantly, reduce until cream is thick and of a sauce-like consistency, approximately 5 minutes. Add diced red bell pepper and chipped butter, 2-3 pats at a time, swirling pan constantly over burner. Do not stir with a spoon, as butter will break down and separate if hot spots develop in the pan. Continue adding butter until all is incorporated. Remove from heat, add parsley and season to taste using salt and pepper. Gently fold in cooked fettuccine and serve. May be chilled and served as a cold pasta salad.

PREP TIME: 45 minutes   SERVES: 6

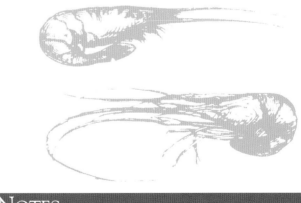

NOTES

_____

_____

_____

_____

_____

_____

SUGARCANE FESTIVAL
New Iberia, Louisiana

It is a celebration of the symbol perhaps most associated with Louisiana and its people; a celebration of an industry critical to the people and economic future of the state. It is the Sugarcane Festival in New Iberia, Louisiana, and it's one that everyone should visit.

Sugarcane farming is the most lucrative industry of Iberia Parish, bringing millions of dollars into the area each year. Fields of vibrant green stalks are growing as far as the eye can see during the growing season until the farmers begin harvesting this sweet crop. It is this important industry, started in the early 1800s on the magnificent plantations which still dot the landscape, that is celebrated each September.

The people of the parish and many surrounding areas come out to a weekend of festivities which are wide ranging. When it is festival time in Iberia Parish, you can be assured of a good time. The weekend before the festival, participants can enter the "Sugar Cane Fun Run" or the "Sweetest Bike Ride in the South," which winds its cyclists through acres of sugar cane.

The festival weekend kicks off with a Sugar Symposium featuring subjects ranging from the history of sugarcane in Louisiana to the impact of politics and lobbying. The real fun kicks off with Farmer's Day when the entire community comes out dressed in farmers' attire. After the traditional Blessing of the Crop, visitors can participate in the Sugar Cookery Contest, Livestock Show, and Quilt and Photography Show. The exciting street fair takes place throughout the afternoons each day of the festival as a highlight for the youngsters.

Other festival attractions include a boat parade, fireworks display, children's parade, livestock auction, and the traditional fais-do-do, where you can't help but kick up your heals to the great Cajun music.

This festival honors the sugarcane industry, which brings almost $2 billion dollars per year into the state. It especially honors the local growers of Iberia Parish who even ride in their own parade on the last day of the festival. The setting of this great gathering is truly Cajun and the Parish of Iberia, with its swamps, bayous, galleries, and breathtaking antebellum homes, is filled with Southern charm.

Lagniappe

Iberia Parish is situated just south of the Acadian city of Lafayette. It is known as the sweetest, saltiest and spiciest place on earth — a name most fitting because of its sugarcane, salt domes, and famous McIlhenny Tabasco sauce.

There is much to do and see without ever leaving the parish. A must see is Avery Island, home to the McIlhenny Tabasco Company which is recognized world wide. You can tour the bottling facility and see just how this spicy sauce is manufactured. The impressive, 200-acre Jungle Gardens are also located on Avery Island. You will also not want to miss touring the beautiful antebellum homes of the parish. My personal favorite is a toss up between Shadows on the Teche in New Iberia and Live Oak Gardens just down the street. For accommodations during your stay, consider one of the many bed-and-breakfast options. La Maison du Teche, a restored Victorian home overlooking Bayou Teche, is one good choice along with leRosier located in downtown New Iberia. You may wish to continue straight ahead into Cade, Louisiana and visit Bruce Foods Corporation, manufacturers of my favorite hot sauce, Louisiana Gold.

Travel on Highway 90 and take Exit 14 to New Iberia. For more information about the festival, call the Iberia Parish Tourist Commission at (318) 365-1540.

Photo: Bill Castel, Heritage Photography
Chef John Folse and Buckley Kessler. Clockwise from bottom left: Pralines, Pain Perdu and a platter of raw sugar.

Cora Texas BBQ Spareribs

INGREDIENTS FOR SAUCE:

4 tbsps butter

1 cup diced onions

1 cup diced celery

1 cup diced yellow bell pepper

1/4 cup diced garlic

1 cup chopped tomatoes

1 cup tomato sauce

1 cup water

1 tsp cloves

1 tsp cinnamon

1 tsp cumin

1 tsp mustard seed

1/4 cup Creole mustard

juice of one lemon

1/2 cup brown sugar

salt and black pepper

Louisiana Gold Pepper Sauce

1/2 cup root beer

1/2 cup Southern Comfort

METHOD:

In a 10-inch cast iron skillet, melt butter over medium-high heat. Add onions, celery, bell pepper and garlic. Saute 3-5 minutes or until vegetables are wilted. Add tomatoes, tomato sauce and water. Blend well until all ingredients are incorporated. Add cloves, cinnamon, cumin and mustard seed. Blend in mustard, lemon juice and brown sugar. Pour in root beer and Souther Comfort. Be careful as liquor will ignite on an open flame. Allow flame to extinguish itself. Season to taste using salt, pepper and Louisiana Gold. Set aside and keep warm.

INGREDIENTS FOR SPARERIBS:

5-6 pounds (2 racks) spareribs or baby back ribs

1/4 cup Liquid Smoke

1/2 cup white wine

2 tbsps Worcestershire sauce

1/2 cup root beer

1/4 cup diced garlic

1 tsp chili powder

1 tsp cumin

1 tsp thyme

1 tsp basil

salt and black pepper

Louisiana Gold Pepper Sauce

METHOD:

Preheat oven to 350 degrees F. Place spareribs, meat side up, in a shallow baking pan. Season to taste using salt and pepper. In a small mixing bowl, combine Liquid Smoke, wine, Worcestershire, root beer, garlic, chili powder, cumin, thyme and basil. Coat spareribs well on both sides with seasoning mixture. Cover with aluminum foil and bake 20 minutes. Remove foil, turn spareribs, meat side down, and bake 20 additional minutes. Baste with Cora Texas Sauce on each side and bake until ribs are tender.

PREP TIME: 1 1/2 hours   SERVES: 6

NOTES

_____

_____

_____

_____

_____

PAIN PERDU
(Lost Bread)

INGREDIENTS:

12 slices stale bread

1 cup oil

½ cup brown sugar

4 eggs

1 tsp vanilla

2 cups milk

powdered sugar

1 tsp cinnamon

1 tsp nutmeg

METHOD:

In a 10-inch cast iron skillet, heat oil over medium-high heat. In a large mixing bowl, beat sugar and eggs. Add vanilla and milk. Dip bread into egg mixture, coating each slice completely. Fry in skillet until golden brown on each side. Top with powdered sugar, cinnamon and nutmeg. As a dessert, try topping with fresh fruit.

PREP TIME: 30 minutes   SERVES: 4

CAJUN PRALINES

INGREDIENTS:

1½ cups sugar

¾ cup light brown sugar, packed

½ cup milk

1 tsp vanilla

¾ stick butter

1½ cups pecans (roasted, optional)

METHOD:

Combine all ingredients and bring to soft ball stage (238-240 degrees F), stirring constantly. Remove from heat. Stir until mixture thickens, becomes creamy and cloudy, and pecans stay suspended in mixture. Spoon out on buttered wax paper, aluminum foil or parchment paper. (When using wax paper, be sure to buffer with newspaper underneath, as hot wax will transfer to whatever is beneath.) *NOTE: To roast pecans, bake them on a sheet pan at 275 degrees for 20 to 25 minutes, until slightly browned and aromatic.*

PREP TIME: 30 minutes   MAKES: 30

NOTES

_____

_____

_____

_____

_____

_____

SPICY MEATBALLS SANS FRUSCINS

INGREDIENTS:

½ pound ground beef
½ pound ground pork
¼ cup minced onions
¼ cup minced celery
¼ cup minced red bell pepper
1 tbsp minced garlic
2 eggs
pinch of thyme
pinch of basil
¾ cup seasoned Italian bread crumbs
¼ cup butter
½ cup ketchup

½ cup barbecue sauce
1 tbsp minced jalapenos
2 tbsps brown sugar
1 tbsp Louisiana cane syrup
1 tbsp red wine vinegar
1 tsp Creole mustard
dash of Worcestershire sauce
salt and cracked black pepper
Louisiana Gold Pepper Sauce
¼ cup chopped parsley

METHOD:

In a large mixing bowl, combine meats, onions, celery, bell pepper, garlic and eggs. Using your hands, blend all ingredients well. Season to taste using salt, pepper, thyme, basil and Louisiana Gold. Continue to mix until seasonings are well blended. Sprinkle in bread crumbs and mix well. Shape into 1-inch meatballs. In a 14-inch cast iron skillet, melt butter over medium-high heat. Add meatballs and brown on all sides. Remove and set aside. Into the same skillet, add ketchup, barbecue sauce, jalapenos, brown sugar, cane syrup and vinegar. Using a wire whisk, stir until well blended. Add mustard, Worcestershire, salt, pepper and Louisiana Gold. Continue to whisk until ingredients begin to simmer. Add cooked meatballs, reduce heat to simmer and cook 15-20 minutes. Sprinkle in fresh parsley. Transfer meatballs and sauce to a chafing dish and serve hot.

PREP TIME: 1 hour   MAKES: 3 dozen

NOTES

_____

_____

_____

_____

_____

SMOTHERED CHICKEN BRULOT

INGREDIENTS:

1 large fryer, cut into serving pieces
½ cup oil
⅓ cup sugar
1½ cups water
1 cup chopped onion
½ cup chopped celery
½ cup chopped bell pepper
¼ cup diced garlic

2 cups chicken stock
1 tsp thyme
1 tsp basil
½ cup sliced green onions
¼ cup chopped parsley
salt and black pepper
Louisiana Gold Pepper Sauce

METHOD:

Season chicken using salt, pepper, thyme and basil. In a cast iron chicken fryer, heat oil over medium-high heat. Add chicken, skin-side down, and cook until golden brown on all sides. Allow mixture to stick to pan, adding a little water each time. While chicken is cooking, melt sugar in an 8-inch cast iron skillet until almost browned. Add water to sugar mixture slowly until brulot is completely dissolved. Set aside. Into chicken skillet, add onions, celery, bell pepper and garlic. Saute 3-5 minutes or until vegetables are wilted. Pour in chicken stock, one ladle at a time, until all is incorporated. Pour sugar/water mixture over chicken, cover and allow to simmer for approximately 15 minutes. Add green onions and parsley. Season to taste using salt, pepper and Louisiana Gold.

PREP TIME: 1½ hours   SERVES: 4

NOTES

_____

_____

_____

_____

_____

_____

MADISONVILLE WOODEN BOAT FESTIVAL
Madisonville, Louisiana

More than 100 wooden boats line the shore of the scenic Tchefuncte (cha-funk-ta) River at the picturesque town of Madisonville each September for the Wooden Boat Festival. The festival, started in 1989, is the largest gathering of antique, classic and contemporary watercraft on the Gulf Coast.

With a Welcome Boaters Day, featuring a second-line dance to greet the arriving boats, the three-day festival gets into high gear. The beautiful line up of boats, including sail, power, rowing and steam, can be seen traveling down the river for great distances as they make their way to the viewing area.

This unique festival features a marine flea market, where visitors can buy or sell used equipment, and several workshops and demonstrations on boat building. Some are offered just for children. A festival highlight is the Quick and Dirty Boat Building Contest where participants build boats and try to make them seaworthy enough to cross the finish line. Great music, street dancing and gourmet food are also an integral part of this festival.

The Wooden Boat Festival is sponsored as a fund-raiser by the Lake Ponchartrain Basin Maritime Museum for the construction and development of a maritime museum. The museum is slated to focus on education of the maritime industry in St. Tammany Parish, an industry that has played a vital role in the cultural history of the area. The Madisonville area was at one time not only a local port, but an international port handling exports and imports from South and Central America.

The charming, historic town of Madisonville is the ideal backdrop for a festival honoring the maritime industry. Its location, right on the beautiful Tchefuncte River and directly across from Lake Ponchartrain, sets it apart and makes it a must see stop on your festival tour.

Lagniappe

Madisonville is conveniently located on the north shore of Lake Ponchartrain across the world's longest bridge. It is situated off of I-12 between Baton Rouge and Slidell. It is one of several communities along the Louisiana Scenic Byways and features shopping, dining, water recreation and overnight accommodations, including the charming Magnolia House Bed & Breakfast. Get a great meal and enjoy a beautiful view of the river at Friends on the Tchefuncte Restaurant. Lodging, shopping and dining opportunities are also available in the nearby communities of Abita Springs, Covington, Mandeville and Slidell. Travel on I-12 and Exit at Madisonville or cross the Ponchartrain Causeway from New Orleans and Exit at Madisonville. For more information about the festival, call the St. Tammany Parish Tourist & Convention Commission at (800) 634-9443 or (504) 898-2029.

Photo: Bill Castel, Heritage Photography
Chef John Folse and Don Scafidi. Clockwise from bottom left: Blue Max Punch and Pickled Vegetables.

CRABMEAT CHEESECAKE WITH NANTUA SAUCE

INGREDIENTS FOR SAUCE:

2 whole cooked or live crabs
$^1/_2$ cup butter
3 cups water
$^1/_2$ cup brandy
1 bouquet garni (3 parsley sprigs, 3 thyme sprigs,
    1 bay leaf and 10 peppercorns tied in cheesecloth)
1 chopped onion

2 chopped carrots
1 garlic clove, minced
$^1/_4$ cup tomato sauce
1 cup shellfish stock
$^1/_2$ cup heavy whipping cream
salt and black pepper
Louisiana Gold Pepper Sauce

METHOD:

Preheat oven to 350 degrees F. Crack crab and reserve juices. Place crab shells in roasting pan. Roast until aromatic, approximately 20 minutes. In the bottom of a 10-inch cast iron skillet, melt butter over medium-high heat. Add crab shells, water, brandy, bouquet garni, onion, carrots, garlic, tomato sauce and stock. Bring to a rolling boil, reduce heat to simmer until liquid is reduced to $^1/_2$ cup, stirring occasionally, about $^1/_2$ hour. Strain. Add cream to cooking liquid and simmer until reduced to $^3/_4$ cup, stirring occasionally, about 10 minutes. Season to taste using salt, pepper and Louisiana Gold. Keep warm.

INGREDIENTS FOR CHEESECAKE:

1 cup jumbo lump crab
6 ounces cream cheese
2 large eggs
$^1/_2$ cup sliced green onions
1 tbsp chopped, seeded tomato

1 small garlic clove
$1^1/_2$ tsps minced fresh dill
$1^1/_2$ tsps fresh lemon juice
salt and black pepper
$^1/_2$ cup chilled unsalted butter, cut into pieces

METHOD:

Butter four 2/3-cup souffle dishes. Using an electric mixer, beat cream cheese in medium bowl until fluffy. Add eggs and beat until thoroughly incorporated. Mix in green onions, tomato, garlic, dill and lemon juice. Stir in crabmeat. Season to taste with salt and pepper. Divide mixture evenly among dishes. Bake until centers are set, about 30 minutes. Cool slightly. Run a sharp knife around sides of cups to loosen cheesecakes. Place one on each plate. Bring sauce to simmer. Gradually add butter, whisking constantly until it is melted. Do not boil. Season to taste with salt and pepper. Spoon sauce over cheesecakes.

PREP TIME: $1^1/_2$ hours   SERVES: 4

NOTES

_____

_____

_____

PICKLED OKRA

INGREDIENTS:

2 pounds fresh small okra
1 cup white vinegar
¼ cup water
2 tsps salt, uniodized
1 tsp dill seed

1 tsp celery seed
2 cloves garlic
1 tsp mustard seed
1 hot green or red pepper, sliced

METHOD:

Wash okra and pack lengthwise tightly in four 1-pint sterilized jars. Bring to a boil the vinegar, water and salt. Add all seasonings to okra in jars and cover with hot vinegar mixture. Seal. Allow 2 or 3 weeks to pickle properly. Serve cold.

PREP TIME: 30 minutes   MAKES: 4 pints

PICKLED ONIONS

INGREDIENTS:

7 quarts onions
2 cups salt
7 cups vinegar
4 tsps celery seed
4 tsps mustard seed

3 tsps turmeric
5 cups sugar
7 cups water
1 (4-ounce) jar sliced pimentos

METHOD:

Peel onions and slice. Add salt, cover and let stand at room temperature for several hours to wilt onions or refrigerate overnight to retain crispness. Drain and rinse off salt thoroughly. Heat vinegar, celery seed, mustard seed, turmeric, sugar, water and pimento. Add onions and boil about 45 minutes or 1 hour, until tender to your taste. Pack in jars and seal while hot. May be eaten anytime, but best when allowed to stand 1-2 months. Serve cold.

PREP TIME: 30 minutes   MAKES: 8 quarts

NOTES

_____

_____

_____

_____

_____

_____

SPINACH ROCKEFELLER ROULADES

INGREDIENTS:

1 (10-ounce) package cooked frozen spinach, thawed
6 (4-inch) squares frozen puff pastry
$^1/_2$ cup melted butter
$^1/_2$ cup minced onions
$^1/_4$ cup minced celery
$^1/_4$ cup minced red bell pepper
$^1/_4$ cup minced yellow bell pepper
1 tbsp chopped garlic

1 tbsp finely diced jalapeno peppers
$^1/_4$ cup diced tasso ham
2 tbsps flour
$^1/_4$ cup heavy whipping cream
$^1/_4$ cup Monterey Jack cheese, grated
salt and black pepper
Louisiana Gold Pepper Sauce
1 egg yolk, whipped

METHOD:

Preheat oven to 375 degrees F. You may purchase puff pastry squares in either full-sheet or 4-inch sections in the frozen food section of your local supermarket. Keep frozen until ready to use. In a 4-quart cast iron dutch oven, heat butter over medium-high heat. Add onions, celery, bell peppers, garlic, jalapenos and tasso. Saute 3-5 minutes or until vegetables are wilted. Squeeze the excess water from the spinach and add to the vegetable mixture. Blend well and heat thoroughly, approximately 3-5 minutes. Sprinkle in flour and stir into the spinach mixture. Add heavy whipping cream and cheese. Season to taste using salt, pepper and Louisiana Gold. When cheese is completely melted, remove from heat and allow to cool. This mixture is better if prepared one day in advance, allowing the seasonings to develop. Remove the puff pastry squares from the freezer and allow to thaw slightly, 5-10 minutes. Spoon approximately 2 tablespoons of the spinach filling into the center of the pastry square and spread evenly from end to end. Roll, jelly roll-style, sealing the spinach mixture into the center of the puff pastry. Make sure that the seam-end is sealed well to keep from opening during the cooking process. Place the roll, seam side down, on a large baking sheet and continue until all of the roulades are stuffed. Brush the top lightly with egg. Bake until pastry is golden brown and cooked throughout, approximately 15-20 minutes. To serve, you may wish to slice in $^1/_2$-inch slices as an hors d'ouvres or cut each roll in half and serve two pieces as an appetizer.

PREP TIME: $1^1/_2$ hours   SERVES: 6-8

NOTES

_____

_____

_____

_____

_____

MELANGE OF SMOKED SEAFOODS

INGREDIENTS:

³/₄ cup olive oil

¹/₄ cup balsamic vinegar

1 tbsp Steen's cane syrup

¹/₂ cup dry white wine

1 tbsp dried thyme

1 tbsp dried basil

1 tbsp dried tarragon

1 tbsp cracked black pepper

¹/₄ cup chopped garlic

salt

1 tbsp Louisiana Gold Pepper Sauce

METHOD:

Select an assortment of fresh Louisiana seafoods. I suggest catfish fillets, speckled trout, peeled and deveined jumbo shrimp, oysters on the half shell or any seafood to your liking. Clean and set aside. Preheat home-style smoker according to manufacturer's directions. Pre-soak pecan or hickory chips in water. You may wish to substitute a bottle of Barq's root beer in place of the water for a really unique flavor. In a large mixing bowl, combine all of the above ingredients and blend well to incorporate flavors. Place a teaspoon of the marinade over each oyster in the shell and all remaining seafood should be placed in the bowl along with the marinade. Turn the ingredients once or twice to coat the seafoods well. Allow to marinate at room temperature 15-20 minutes. When ready to smoke, place the wood chips over the hot coals and smoke the seafoods and oysters until cooked and fish is flaky, approximately 20-30 minutes. Remove and serve hot or cold along with your favorite dipping sauce.

PREP TIME: 1 hour   SERVES: According to ingredients

BLUE MAX PUNCH

INGREDIENTS:

4 cups ginger ale

2 cups orange or pineapple juice

2 cups champagne

1 cup Blue Curacao

crushed ice

METHOD:

In a large punch bowl, combine all ingredients until well blended. Pour over crushed ice in champagne glasses.

PREP TIME: 30 minutes   SERVES: 4

NOTES

_____

_____

_____

_____

_____

_____

Chapter Eight
October

Celtic Nations Heritage Festival
International Rice Festival
Pepper Festival
Sunshine Festival
The Gumbo Festival
Washington Parish Free Fair Festival
Yambilee Festival

CELTIC NATIONS HERITAGE FESTIVAL
City Park, New Orleans, Louisiana

Experience first hand the rich cultural legacy of our Celtic forbearers as entertainers, craftsmen, artisans and athletes celebrate the culture of the Celtic nations — Ireland, Scotland, Wales, Cornwall, Brittany, Isle of Man and Galicia in Northern Spain. For two days each fall at Marconi Meadows in New Orleans' City Park, this festival reestablishes authentic ties with the Celtic Nations and the thousands in Louisiana who claim a Celtic heritage.

Started in 1991, the dates of the Celtic Nations Heritage Festival coincide with Louisiana's Celtic Heritage Week. It is a festival filled with uncommon activities certainly unlike most found at other Louisiana festivals — Irish and Scottish dance workshops, the Currach Regatta, and athletic events which include the Caber Toss and Hammer Throw, just to name a few.

You will undoubtedly be inspired to kick up your heels when you hear the sounds of bagpipes at the opening parade each day. Other entertainers include internationally-acclaimed artists who play authentic, traditional instruments from their native lands.

The Currach Regatta provides a rare opportunity for visitors to the festival to glimpse a living part of western Ireland's maritime history. Teams from the U.S. and Ireland compete along the shores of the City Park Lagoon in traditional Irish fishing boats known as "currachs," which are 23 feet long and made of tar-covered canvas stretched over a wooden frame.

Children enjoy the arts and crafts in a special Children's Pavilion, while sports enthusiasts partake in highland games including the caber toss, sheaf toss, Scottish hammer throw and Irish weight throw. Genealogists are on hand to provide information on Celtic family history. Artisans from the Celtic countries demonstrate tartan weaving, Irish linen making and Welsh "Love Spoon" carving. At the dog exhibition, you can find out anything you ever wanted to know about over twenty Celtic breeds like the Scottish Terrier, Brittany Spaniel, Irish Wolf Hound or Irish Setter, to name a few.

We must not forget the authentic Celtic foods of the festival. From corned beef and cabbage to the Iced Irish Whiskey Truffle, the featured foods are fantastic and make you wish you were Celtic, even if you're not.

Lagniappe

This festival is held in the heart of New Orleans at City Park. Once a swampy oak-filled forest, City Park has evolved into the fifth largest urban park in the nation, encompassing 1,500 acres. Home to the New Orleans Museum of Art and the largest collection of mature live oaks in the world, City Park also offers golf, tennis, canoe and paddle boat rentals and year-round freshwater fishing.

For your dining, lodging and entertainment options, the city of New Orleans features hundreds of choices. For dining, you may choose a formal Jazz brunch at acclaimed Commander's Palace or poboys at Maspero's in the French Quarter. Emeril's, Bayona's, K-Paul's and Uglesich's Restaurant are among some of the finest in all of New Orleans. The Bienville House and the elegant Royal Sonesta Hotel are always good lodging choices.

Travel on I-10 and take the City Park Exit. Tickets are $7 for adults and $5 for children. For more information about the festival, call (504) 891-5484.

Photo: José L. Garcia, II
Martin Schreiber, Caledonian Society of Baton Rouge. Clockwise from bottom left: Baked Corned Beef, Celtic Biscuits and Spring Vegetables.

BAKED CORNED BEEF

INGREDIENTS:

1 (3-4 pound) corned beef brisket
1 package Zatarain's crab boil
2-3 bay leaves
1 cup chopped onions
¼ cup chopped garlic
½ cup black peppercorns

1 tbsp prepared yellow mustard
¼ cup brown sugar
1 tbsp cane syrup
1 (15-ounce) can spiced peaches
whole cloves

METHOD:

Cover corned beef with water flavored with crab boil. Add bay leaves, onions, garlic and peppercorns, and bring mixture to a low boil. Cover and cook until meat is very tender, approximately 2 hours. Drain meat and remove all fat. Preheat oven to 325 degrees F. Place corned beef in a large baking pan. In a small mixing bowl, make a paste of mustard, brown sugar, cane syrup and spiced peach juice. Spread over corned beef until completely covered. Stud the corned beef at 2-inch intervals with the whole cloves. Surround corned beef with peaches and bake for approximately 1 hour, basting frequently with spiced peach syrup.

PREP TIME: 5 hours   SERVES: 6-8

CHIVE POTATO SAUCE FOR SALMON

INGREDIENTS:

1 potato cut in ½-inch cubes
5 ounces hot chicken stock

2 tbsps sliced chives
salt and pepper

METHOD:

Boil potatoes in lightly salted water until tender. Strain and place potato in food processor. Add stock in two additions. Make sure to puree completely before adding second addition. Do not over mix. Add chives, salt and pepper. Serve under poached salmon.

PREP TIME: 30 minutes   SERVES: 6

NOTES

_____
_____
_____
_____
_____
_____

POACHED SALMON

INGREDIENTS FOR COURTBOUILLON:

16 ounces dry white wine
2 cups water
1 cup carrots, peeled and diced
1/2 cup white of leek, diced
1/2 cup diced onions
1/4 cup diced celery
salt

1 clove
5 sprigs parsley
1 sprig thyme
1/2 bay leaf
5 white peppercorns, crushed
3 coriander seeds

METHOD:

In a large sauce pan, bring the white wine and water to a boil. Add all remaining ingredients, except for salt and allow to simmer for 10 minutes. Season with salt and strain through a fine sieve.

INGREDIENTS FOR POACHED SALMON:

6 (4-ounce) salmon fillets
Courtbouillon liquid

Chive Potato Sauce (see recipe)

METHOD:

Bring liquid to a rolling boil. Place salmon in a 9" x 13" baking pan. When ready to serve, pour boiling liquid over the fish. Cover quickly with clear wrap and allow to set 5-7 minutes or until done. Place poached fillet in center of plate and top with warm potato sauce.

PREP TIME: 30 minutes   SERVES: 6

NOTES

_____

_____

_____

_____

_____

_____

CELTIC BISCUITS

INGREDIENTS:

4 1/2 cups unbleached flour

2 tsps baking powder

1 tsp baking soda

3 tbsps sugar

1 cup cold butter

1 cup currants

1/4 cup Irish whiskey

1 tbsp caraway seeds

1 1/2 cups milk

METHOD:

Preheat oven to 350 degrees F. In a large mixing bowl, stir flour, baking powder, baking soda and sugar together. Cut butter into small pieces and add to flour. Using a pastry blender, blend mixture until grainy. Place currants and Irish whiskey in a small cast iron sauce pan and bring to a rolling boil. Reduce heat and simmer 2 minutes. Remove from heat and cool. Add soaked currants, caraway seeds and 1/4 cup of milk to flour mixture. Mix with your hands until dough holds together. Wrap dough in plastic wrap and refrigerate at least 1 hour. Roll out dough on floured board to 1 3/4-inch thickness. Cut with clover-shaped biscuit cutter and place on baking sheets lined with parchment paper. Brush remaining milk over top of biscuits. Bake until lightly browned, about 20 minutes.

PREP TIME: 2 hours   MAKES: 1 dozen

NOTES

_____

_____

_____

_____

_____

_____

IRISH APPLE CAKE

INGREDIENTS:

2 1/2 cups flour

1/3 tsp baking powder

3/4 cup butter

2/3 cup sugar

1 egg, beaten

1/2 cup milk

1 green apple

1 red apple

1 tsp ground cloves

1 egg, beaten

1/2 cup powdered sugar

1/4 cup dark brown sugar

2 cups whipped cream

METHOD:

Preheat oven to 350 degrees F. Into a large mixing bowl, sift flour and baking powder. Rub in butter with your fingertips until mixture resembles texture of bread crumbs. Add 1/2 cup of sugar and mix well. Make well in center of flour mixture, and mix in beaten egg and enough milk to make a soft dough. Divide dough in half. Put 1/2 in greased pie plate and pat it out to cover the bottom completely. Peel, core and chop apples. Place them on dough, with cloves and remaining sugar to taste. Roll out remaining dough on lightly floured board and fit dough on top of apples. (You may need to do a bit of patchwork if it breaks.) Press edges together and cut a slit through top crust. Beat remaining egg and brush onto crust. Bake until cooked through and nicely browned, approximately 40 minutes. Dust with powdered sugar and serve warm with dark brown sugar and softly whipped cream.

PREP TIME: 1 1/2 hours   SERVES: 6

NOTES

_____

_____

_____

_____

_____

_____

INTERNATIONAL RICE FESTIVAL
Crowley, Louisiana

Since the early 1930s, an estimated seven million people have traveled to downtown Crowley, Louisiana during the third weekend each October to take part in a celebration which hails the importance of rice and emphasizes its place in the world economy. Crowley shares with most of southwest Louisiana a tradition of Indian and Acadian influences. The importance of the rice industry here is a reflection of these cultures.

The first day of the festival is traditionally recognized as "Children's Day," with activities including the crowning of the junior King and Queen, a Rice Eating Contest, and the Children's Parade. The day is closed with the Queen's Ball held where else but the International Rice Festival Building.

The second day of the festival kicks off with two entertainment platforms becoming stages for the best of musical talent in the area. The day is filled with unique events like the Livestock Show, Acadian Accordion Contest, Fiddler's Contest, Frog Derby, street dances and the highlight of the day, the Grand Parade. Of course, no festival would be complete without a cooking contest, and the requirement of this one is that each entry must feature rice as the main ingredient. The mayor and city council members even participate in the many festival contests including the rice sack sewing contest.

This festival gives a great view into the agricultural past as area farmers demonstrate harvesting and processing techniques using equipment of days gone by. They provide a great way for visitors to catch a glimpse into the cultural and industrial past of the area.

Crowley is proud of the distinguished guests which have been attracted to the festival. They boast about the attendance of former Presidents Harry Truman and John F. Kennedy, Senator Barry Goldwater and entertainer Ed McMahon.

The festival is praised by rice industry producers and strongly supported each year by the industry.

So, travel to festival country in southwest Louisiana to take in yet another one of this state's traditions — the International Rice Festival — which pays tribute to that all important ingredient to so many great Louisiana dishes.

Lagniappe

Crowley is located just west of Lafayette along I-10. This southwest Louisiana town is only 20 miles from the Acadian city and less than an hour's drive from Lake Charles to its west. While visiting the festival, you may want to take in the sites at the Rice Museum located on Highway 90 west of Crowley. For a cozy night's sleep, you may wish to visit the Creole Rose Manor bed-and-breakfast, circa 1898, in the neighboring town of Jennings. While in Jennings, visit the Ziegler Museum and take time to stop for lunch at the Boudin King Restaurant, owned by Ellis Cormier. Or you may try the Maison Da Boval, circa 1892, in Rayne — the frog capital of the world. If you wish to travel east to Lafayette, see top attractions such as Acadian Village Vermilionville and the Acadian Cultural Center Jean Lafitte National Park. Lake Charles to the west is a charming southwest Louisiana city featuring marshes, winding rivers and stunning beaches.

Travel on I-10 to the Crowley exit. Crowley is one mile from the Interstate. For more information about the festival, call (504) 783-3067.

Photo: Bill Castel, Heritage Photography
Chef John Folse and Wayne Garber. Clockwise from bottom left: Red Beans, Rice and Sausage Gumbo, Raised Calas (Rice Cakes), Crawfish Risotto and Seafood Jambalaya Rice Salad.

RISOTTO

INGREDIENTS:

2 cups Arborio rice

1/2 cup chopped artichoke hearts

1 cup crawfish tails

2 tbsps saffron

2 cups water

1/4 cup olive oil

1 cup chopped onions

1 cup chopped celery

1 cup chopped bell pepper

1/4 cup diced garlic

4 cups hot shellfish stock

1 tsp fresh thyme, chopped

1 tsp fresh basil, chopped

salt and black pepper

Louisiana Gold Pepper Sauce

METHOD:

Dissolve saffron in water. Set aside. In a 10-inch cast iron skillet, heat oil over medium-high heat. Add onions, celery, bell pepper and garlic. Saute 3-5 minutes or until vegetables are wilted. Add rice and saute 5-10 minutes until all grains are well coated. Pour in saffron liquid, blending well into rice mixture. Add hot stock, one ladle at a time, stirring occasionally until the liquid is absorbed. Continue adding stock and stirring until rice is cooked and creamy in appearance. Add artichokes and crawfish, blending well into the cooked risotto. Cook until heated thoroughly and season to taste using thyme, basil, salt, pepper and Louisiana Gold.

PREP TIME: 1 hour   SERVES: 6

NOTES

_____

_____

_____

_____

_____

RED BEANS, RICE & SAUSAGE GUMBO

INGREDIENTS:

3 cups cooked red kidney beans, reserve stock
1 cup cooked rice
2 cups heavy smoked sausage, sliced
1 cup diced tasso
1 cup diced andouille
1 cup vegetable oil
1 cup flour
1 cup chopped onions
1 cup chopped celery

1 cup chopped bell pepper
¼ cup diced garlic
3 quarts reserved stock or water
1 cup chopped tomatoes
1 tsp fresh thyme, chopped
1 tsp fresh basil, chopped
salt and black pepper
Louisiana Gold Pepper Sauce

METHOD:

In a 5-quart cast iron dutch oven, heat oil over medium-high heat. Add flour and, using a wire whisk, stir constantly until dark brown roux is achieved. Add onions, celery, bell pepper and garlic. Saute 3-5 minutes or until vegetables are wilted. Add smoked sausage, tasso and andouille. Pour in stock, one ladle at a time, until all is incorporated. Add beans, bring to a rolling boil and cook 30 minutes. Add tomatoes and season to taste using thyme, basil, salt, pepper and Louisiana Gold. Add rice blending well into soup.

PREP TIME: 1 hour   SERVES: 6

NOTES

_____
_____
_____
_____
_____
_____

SEAFOOD JAMBALAYA RICE SALAD

INGREDIENTS:

2 cups cooked rice

1 cup mayonnaise

$^1/_2$ cup Creole mustard

1 cup chopped tomatoes

1 cup chopped Bermuda onions

1 tbsp fresh thyme, chopped

1 tbsp fresh basil, chopped

1 cup crawfish tails

1 cup jumbo lump crabmeat

1 cup (60-90 count) boiled shrimp

$^1/_2$ cup diced ham

$^1/_2$ cup sliced smoked sausage

$^1/_2$ cup sliced green onions

$^1/_4$ cup chopped parsley

salt and black pepper

Louisiana Gold Pepper Sauce

METHOD:

In a large mixing bowl, place rice. Add mayonnaise, mustard, tomatoes and onions. Blend well until all is incorporated. Season to taste using thyme, basil, salt, pepper and Louisiana Gold. Add seafoods, ham and sausage. Mix until thoroughly blended. Add green onions and parsley. Refrigerate for 2 hours and serve on lettuce leaves.

PREP TIME: 30 minutes   SERVES: 6

NOTES

_____

_____

_____

_____

_____

RAISED CALAS (RICE CAKES)

INGREDIENTS:

1 cup long grain white rice
1½ cups cold water
1 tsp salt
½ tsp butter
1 package dry yeast
½ cup warm water
3 large eggs, well beaten

¼ cup sugar
¼ tsp freshly grated nutmeg
½ tsp salt
1¼ cups flour
2 cups vegetable oil
confectioners sugar

METHOD:

In a 2-quart cast iron sauce pan, combine water, salt and butter. Bring mixture to a rolling boil and add rice. Reduce heat to simmer, cover and cook 30 minutes. Do not remove cover or stir rice during the cooking process. When done, stir rice and place in a large mixing bowl. Using the back of a wooden spoon, mash rice and allow to cool. Dissolve yeast in water. Add to rice and beat thoroughly with a spoon for approximately 2 minutes. Cover the bowl with a towel and set in a warm place to rise overnight. Add eggs, sugar, nutmeg, salt and flour to rice mixture. Stir mixture well and cover bowl again. Set in a warm place to rise for 30 minutes. In a 14-inch cast iron skillet, heat oil over medium-high heat. Drop the rice batter by heaping tablespoons into the hot oil. Deep fry cakes, 4 to 5 at a time, until golden brown on all sides. Remove and place on drain board. Top each cake with confectioners sugar. Serve hot.

PREP TIME: 30 minutes   SERVES: 4

NOTES

_____

_____

_____

_____

_____

_____

BOUDIN BLANC

Boudin blanc, the Cajun pork and rice sausage, is without a doubt the best known sausage in South Louisiana. Its less famous sister, boudin rouge, though made in the same fashion, is colored by the addition of pork blood into the dish and is considered a rare delicacy. The boudin blanc of Louisiana is quite different from the milk-based boudin of France. The Louisiana version is much more spicy and normally includes rice as a main ingredient. Boudin rouge originated from the boudin noir or blood pudding of France and was particularly enjoyed around Christmas time. These well seasoned by-products of the boucherie are a delight to savor and well worth the extra effort. The boudins are normally served cold as a Cajun canape; however, in our house it was best eaten hot as a breakfast item.

INGREDIENTS:

10 pounds Boston butt, cubed

2 pounds pork liver

1 pound green onions

1 pound parsley

6 tbsps cayenne pepper

4 tbsps black pepper

8 ounces salt

6 pounds cooked white rice

$^1/_2$ gallon cold water

1 cup chopped pimentos

75 feet sausage casing

METHOD:

Using a home-style meat grinder, alternately grind meat, liver, green onions and parsley. Once the raw ingredients have been ground, season with salt and peppers. Place the mixture into a large mixing bowl then add the cooked white rice, water and pimentos. Using both hands, blend the meat and rice mixture until all is incorporated. Using a sausage stuffer, fill the casing, twisting into 6-inch links. Once all has been stuffed, place the boudin in a home-style steamer, cover and cook for approximately 45 minutes or until sausage is firm and fully cooked. Makes approximately 125 links.

PREP TIME: 3 hours   MAKES: 6-10 pounds boudin

NOTES

_____

_____

_____

_____

_____

_____

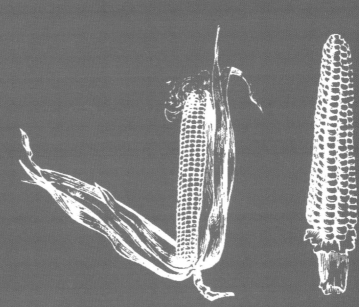

PEPPER FESTIVAL
St. Martinville, Louisiana

Along scenic Bayou Teche, brave festival lovers can test their heat endurance and have some spicy fun at the annual Pepper Festival sponsored by the Kiwanis Club of St. Martinville. Visitors to the festival gather at the magnificent Evangeline Oak which stands on the bayou's bank.

Nestled among the oaks and mid-19th Century buildings of this historic, picturesque town on a Sunday each October, the Pepper Festival begins with a fun walk and run and continues until sundown with plenty of food and entertainment. A celebrity chef will cook up samples of foods featuring many brands of pepper sauce made in the area. Only a few stomachs will be able to endure the annual pepper eating contest in which local winners have been known to eat over 200 of the hottest varieties of fiery peppers including habaneras, cayennes and jalapenos.

Pepper manufacturers showcase their pepper products and offer many varieties of sample dishes for the visitors. You should also try a portion of the jambalaya or gumbo — topped with a few dashes of the spicy sauce, of course.

Local crafters demonstrate their techniques and display items which pay tribute to the festival's namesake in one way or another. A special area of the festival is designated for kids where you can see the youngsters playing street games and dancing to the festival music. Don't forget to look for the Pepper Festival Queen who is always on hand to greet visitors.

This Louisiana festival celebrates the spicy, fiery hot peppers, and their somewhat milder counterparts, which are so linked to the foods of the state. Spending a Sunday along Bayou Teche in this quaint, Cajun town during the annual Pepper Festival is a great way to spice up your life.

Lagniappe

St. Martinville is in the heart of Cajun Country and offers a true look into Louisiana's colorful and cultural past. In the center of the town square is one of the oldest and most historic churches in America, St. Martin de Tours Catholic Church on S. Main Street. The 1700s structure is also the gravesite of the heroine of Cajun Country, Longfellow's Evangeline.

You may choose to lodge and dine at the historic Old Castillo Hotel or travel to the nearby Acadian City of Lafayette, only a few miles to the north. There you can find authentic Cajun fare and music at Catfish Town USA or The Original Mulate's Cajun Restaurant. The bustling city of Lafayette also offers an abundance of family activities.

Travel on Highway 90 and exit at St. Martinville, travel east to Bayou Teche. Festival admission is only $1. For more information about the festival, call the St. Martinville Chamber of Commerce at (318) 394-7578.

Photo: José L. Garcia, II
Clockwise from bottom left: Pepper-Laced Pork Roast, Bowls of Roasted Red Pepper and Crab Soup.

ROASTED RED PEPPER AND CRAB SOUP

INGREDIENTS:

4 roasted red bell peppers, seeded and chopped
1 pound claw crabmeat
$^1/_4$ cup butter
1 cup chopped onions
$^1/_2$ cup chopped celery
$^1/_4$ cup diced garlic

$^1/_4$ cup flour
2 quarts chicken stock
6 ounces heavy whipping cream
salt and cayenne pepper
2 tbsps chopped parsley
Louisiana Gold Pepper Sauce

METHOD:

To roast peppers, place the peppers directly over an open gas flame, turning frequently as the skin becomes black and blistered from the heat. This blackening will not cause the pepper to taste burned but will give it a high-quality roasted taste. Once the peppers are totally blackened, place in a brown paper bag and seal the top tightly allowing the peppers to steam for 5-10 minutes. Bring the bag over to a sink and remove the peppers, one at a time, washing the blistered skin off the pepper under cold running water. Remove the stems and seeds. Continue until all peppers are done. (If a gas range is not available, place the peppers on a cookie sheet in a 400 degree F oven until the peppers are blackened and blistered and follow the above process.) In a 12-quart cast iron dutch oven, melt butter over medium-high heat. Reserve one of the chopped roasted peppers for garnish. Add onions, celery, three remaining bell peppers and garlic. Saute 3-5 minutes or until vegetables are wilted. Sprinkle in flour and, using a wire whisk, stir constantly until blond roux is achieved. Add chicken stock, blending well into vegetable mixture. Add cream, bring to a rolling boil and reduce heat to simmer. Allow mixture to cook 30 minutes until thickened. While soup is cooking, puree remaining pepper in a food processor. Remove and set aside for garnish. Fold crabmeat into soup, being careful not to break lumps. Season to taste using salt, pepper and Louisiana Gold. Serve in a large soup bowl and garnish with fresh parsley and roasted red peppers.

PREP TIME: 1 hour   **SERVES:** 6

NOTES

_____
_____
_____
_____
_____
_____

PEPPER-LACED PORK ROAST

INGREDIENTS:

1 (5-6 pound) boneless pork roast
6 chopped garlic cloves
$^1/_2$ cup sliced green onions
1/8 tsp dried thyme
1/8 tsp dried basil
1 tsp salt
1/8 tsp black pepper
$^1/_4$ cup sliced cayenne and jalapeno peppers

$^1/_4$ cup oil
$^1/_2$ cup chopped onions
$^1/_4$ cup chopped celery
$^1/_4$ cup chopped bell pepper
$^1/_4$ cup chopped parsley
1 quart beef stock
Louisiana Gold Pepper Sauce

METHOD:

Preheat oven to 375 degrees F. In a small mixing bowl combine garlic, green onions, thyme, basil, salt and pepper. Pierce holes through the roast and fill each cavity with mixture. Follow with the peppers, leaving approximately $^1/_2$ of pepper exposed. (This will give flavor to the roast.) Season the roast completely with salt, pepper and Louisiana Gold. In a 12-quart cast iron dutch oven, heat oil over medium-high heat. Sear roast in hot oil on both sides. Add onions, celery, bell pepper and beef stock. Cover and bake until tender, approximately $2^1/_2$ hours. Add water if necessary, reserving broth for serving.

PREP TIME: 3 hours   SERVES: 6

NOTES

_____

_____

_____

_____

_____

_____

155

BACON AND ROASTED BELL PEPPER FINGER SANDWICHES

INGREDIENTS:

2 cups roasted red bell peppers, chopped
2 loaves sandwich bread
4 pounds bacon
$^3/_4$ cup minced celery
12 hard boiled eggs, chopped

16 ounces cream cheese
16 ounces mayonnaise
$^1/_2$ cup sliced green onions
salt and black pepper
Louisiana Gold Pepper Sauce

METHOD:

See roasting pepper method on page 154.

Trim the crust off the bread slices and set aside. In a cast iron skillet, fry bacon until crisp. Drain and crumble. In a large mixing bowl, combine bacon, celery, bell pepper, eggs, cream cheese, mayonnaise and green onions. Season to taste using salt, pepper and Louisiana Gold. Spread mixture onto bread and cut into various shapes. Refrigerate prior to serving.

PREP TIME: 30 minutes   MAKES: 80 finger sandwiches

PEPPERED HAM SALAD

INGREDIENTS:

3 cups cooked ham, diced
$^1/_4$ cup minced celery
$^1/_4$ cup minced yellow bell pepper
$^1/_4$ cup minced black olives
2 tbsps minced pimentos
1 tbsp minced jalapeno peppers

2 cups mayonnaise
$^1/_2$ cup sliced green onions
1 tbsp Worcestershire sauce
salt and black pepper
Louisiana Gold Pepper Sauce

METHOD:

In the bowl of a food processor, finely chop cooked ham. Remove and place in a mixing bowl. Add celery, bell pepper, olives, pimentos, jalapeno peppers, mayonnaise and green onions. Using a wooden spoon, blend all ingredients well. Add Worcestershire, salt, pepper and Louisiana Gold. Refrigerate prior to serving. This salad may be used as a sandwich spread or served over crisp lettuce leaves.

PREP TIME: 30 minutes   MAKES: 4 cups

NOTES

_____

_____

_____

ARMADILLO EGGS

INGREDIENTS:

24 jalapeno peppers

$^1/_4$ cup vegetable oil

$^1/_2$ pound crawfish tails, chopped

$^1/_4$ cup minced onions

$^1/_4$ cup minced celery

$^1/_4$ cup minced red bell pepper

$^1/_4$ cup minced garlic

$^1/_4$ tsp lemon juice

salt and black pepper

Louisiana Gold Pepper Sauce

$^1/_2$ cup seasoned Italian bread crumbs

2 cups vegetable oil

eggwash (1 egg, $^1/_2$ cup milk, $^1/_2$ cup water)

1 cup seasoned corn flour

oil for deep frying

METHOD:

Split jalapeno peppers and remove seeds. In a 10-inch cast iron skillet, heat oil over medium high heat. Add onions, celery, bell pepper, garlic and crawfish. Saute 3-5 minutes or until vegetables are wilted. Season to taste using salt, pepper and Louisiana Gold. Remove and sprinkle in bread crumbs until consistency is that of a stuffing. Preheat oil in a home-style fryer such as a Fry Daddy to 375 degrees F. Stuff jalapenos with crawfish stuffing. Prepare eggwash by blending egg, milk and water. Season to taste using salt and pepper. Dredge stuffed-jalapenos in eggwash then into corn flour. Deep fry until golden brown on both sides. Remove and serve warm.

PREP TIME: 30 minutes   SERVES: 6

NOTES

_____

_____

_____

_____

_____

_____

SUNSHINE FESTIVAL
Donaldsonville, Louisiana

Known as the "Gateway to Cajun and Plantation Country," Donaldsonville, Louisiana is located on the west bank of the mighty Mississippi River between Baton Rouge and New Orleans. Once you cross the Sunshine Bridge, you will enter an historic riverfront town boasting a unique cultural heritage coupled with thriving industry.

It is this scenic, Cajun town which serves as host for the annual Sunshine Festival each fall. Featuring activities for all ages, the festival brings folks together from many surrounding parishes to enjoy the fun. Events span from the ever-popular cooking contest where entries include dishes such as alligator sauce piquante, rabbit jambalaya, and other wild game fare, to the traditional live music, arts and crafts and fireworks display. A 5K Fun Run is available to those who wish to show their athletic abilities. A car show of antiques and classics is also a big hit with festival participants.

With a ten-block area closed to traffic, vendors at the Trade Show and Arts and Crafts Show have plenty of room to exhibit their items. A magic show, tug- of-war competition and old-fashioned demolition derby round out the featured events.

Proceeds from the festival are put to good use as they are donated to area civic and community programs. Organizers say it has generated a renewed atmosphere of community spirit and unity in Donaldsonville. This is evident as everyone, locals and visitors alike, are seen having a fun time in the sun at the annual Donaldsonville Sunshine Festival.

Lagniappe

You will not have trouble finding a place to dine while visiting this Louisiana festival, since Donaldsonville is home of Lafitte's Landing, acclaimed restaurant of Chef John Folse. You can't miss the beautiful plantation setting of Lafitte's at the foot of the Sunshine Bridge. Finding a great place to stay is also no problem here, as you are within easy driving distance to the most beautiful plantations in the south, many of which offer bed-and-breakfast accommodations. Nottoway, Oak Alley or Tezcuco plantations are all outstanding choices. If you choose not to stay at one of the plantation homes, you must take the time to tour them. You can enjoy a walking tour of the historic district and relive the days when Donaldsonville served as the Capital of Louisiana. The Cajun Village in nearby Sorrento is also a great stop where you can enjoy a few hot beignets and browse through wonderful Cajun gift shops. Donaldsonville is conveniently located only 35 miles from Baton Rouge and 60 miles from New Orleans.

From I-10, take the Sunshine Bridge Exit, cross the bridge and travel to Donaldsonville. For more information about the festival, call the Donaldsonville Area Chamber of Commerce at (504) 473-4814.

Photo: Bill Castel, Heritage Photography
Chef John Folse and Rosemary Birnbaum. Clockwise from bottom left: A variety of mushrooms, Speckled Belly Mandarin Goose, Pot Roasted Teal Hopping John.

POT-ROASTED TEAL HOPPING JOHN

INGREDIENTS:

6 teal wood ducks
1 cup vegetable oil
2 cups rice
1 cup chopped pecans
¼ cup butter
1 cup chopped onions
1 cup chopped celery
1 cup chopped bell pepper
¼ cup diced garlic
½ cup diced tasso
1 (10-ounce) can blackeyed peas

1 ear of corn, sliced
1 quart reserved teal stock
1 cup tomato sauce
1 tsp fresh thyme, chopped
1 tsp fresh basil, chopped
½ cup sliced green onions
¼ cup chopped parsley
salt and black pepper
Louisiana Gold Pepper Sauce

METHOD:

Debone teal duck and remove breasts. Set aside. In a 2-gallon stock pot, place remaining teal pieces along with 1 onion, quartered, 1 rib of celery, 1 whole head of garlic, thyme, basil, Worcestershire, salt, pepper, Louisiana Gold and water to cover by 2-inches. Bring mixture to a rolling boil, reduce to simmer and cook 30 minutes. Remove from heat, strain and discard vegetables. Reserve approximately 1 quart of liquid. Season teal breasts using thyme, basil, salt, pepper and Louisiana Gold. In a 10-inch cast iron skillet, heat oil over medium-high heat. Add breasts, skin side down, and sear until lightly browned. Remove, drain and set aside. In a 3-quart cast iron dutch oven, melt butter over medium-high heat. Add onions, celery, bell pepper and garlic. Saute 3-5 minutes or until vegetables are wilted. Add tasso, peas and corn. Continue to saute an additional 10 minutes. Add stock, one ladle at a time, until all is incorporated. Add tomato sauce, thyme and basil, blending well into the stock mixture. Season to taste using salt, pepper and Louisiana Gold. Bring mixture to a rolling boil, reduce to simmer and cook 10 minutes. Stir in rice, teal and pecans. Cover, reduce heat to simmer and cook for 30 minutes. Do not remove lid or stir rice during the cooking process. Add green onions and parsley. Serve hot with French bread.

NOTES

_____

_____

_____

_____

_____

_____

SPECKLED-BELLY MANDARIN GOOSE

INGREDIENTS:

3 mandarins, halved

5-7 pound goose, cleaned

$\frac{1}{4}$ cup diced garlic

$\frac{1}{4}$ cup sliced green onions

4 strips raw bacon, chopped

2 ribs celery, sliced

1 carrot, sliced

1 apple, sliced

1 cup seedless grapes

1 potato, sliced

6 oyster mushrooms

salt and black pepper

Louisiana Gold Pepper Sauce

$\frac{1}{2}$ cup grated mandarin peel

METHOD:

Preheat oven to 350 degrees F. In a small mixing bowl, combine garlic, green onions, salt, pepper and Louisiana Gold. Using a paring knife, cut 2-inch vertical slits evenly around the top of the goose and stuff with seasoning mixture and bacon. Season goose evenly inside and out using salt, pepper and Louisiana Gold. Stuff the cavity of the goose with $\frac{1}{2}$ of the celery, carrots, apples, grapes and mandarins. Line the bottom of a cast iron roasting pan with potato slices. Place goose in the pan and surround with remaining vegetables, fruits and mushrooms. Squeeze mandarin juice over the top of the bird. Cover and cook for 2 hours. Remove cover and brown goose for 30 minutes. Garnish with grated mandarin peel.

PREP TIME: 3 hours   SERVES: 6

NOTES

_____

_____

_____

_____

_____

161

GARLIC MASHED POTATOES

INGREDIENTS:

6 garlic cloves

6 potatoes, peeled

3 cups milk

1 cup butter

salt and black pepper

1/4 cup chopped parsley

METHOD:

Rinse potatoes under cold water and cut into 1-inch cubes. In a 3-quart cast iron sauce pot, place milk over medium-high heat. Add potatoes and garlic. Bring mixture to a rolling boil, reduce to simmer and cook until potatoes are tender, but not mushy. Remove and place in a large mixing bowl with butter. Mash potatoes and garlic until desired consistency. Season to taste using salt and pepper. Serve hot and garnish with parsley.

PREP TIME: 30 minutes   SERVES: 6

STUFFED PUMPKINS

INGREDIENTS:

8 (3-inch) pumpkins, hollowed out

1 cup granulated sugar

1/2 tsp salt

1 1/2 cups pumpkin meat

1 (8-ounce) can evaporated milk

2 eggs

2 tsps pumpkin pie spice

1 tsp cinnamon

1 tsp nutmeg

METHOD:

Preheat oven to 425 degrees F. In a large mixing bowl, combine sugar, salt, pumpkin, milk, eggs, pumpkin spice, cinnamon and nutmeg. Blend all ingredients until smooth. Fill each pumpkin with mixture. Place on greased cookie sheet and bake for 15 minutes. Decrease oven temperature to 350 degrees F and bake for 30 additional minutes.

PREP TIME: 1 hour   SERVES: 6

NOTES

_____

_____

_____

_____

_____

_____

162

GRANDMA'S ITALIAN FIG COOKIES

INGREDIENTS:

$2^{1}/_{2}$ cups fig preserves

8 ounces butter

4 ounces sugar

2 tsps vanilla

12 ounces flour

1 egg, beaten

$^{1}/_{4}$ cup milk

METHOD:

Preheat oven to 350 degrees F. In a large mixing bowl, beat butter and sugar until creamy. Add vanilla and blend well into sugar mixture. Sprinkle in flour, one spoon at a time, until dough ball is formed. Place dough on a lightly floured work surface and knead for a few minutes until dough is well formed. Dust the work surface with additional flour and roll dough to 1/8-inch thickness. Using a 3-inch pastry cutter, cut dough into circles until all is used up. Place approximately 2 teaspoons of fig preserves in the center of each circle. In a small mixing bowl, combine egg and milk. Using a pastry brush, paint the eggwash 1/4-inch deep around the pastry circle. Fold the dough over into a half-moon shape and crimp the edges together with a fork. Place the cookies on a baking sheet and pierce the top of each cookie with a fork to create 4 steam holes. Brush the top of the cookie lightly with the remaining eggwash. Bake for 20-25 minutes or until golden brown. Powdered sugar may be added as a garnish.

PREP TIME: 1 hour   MAKES: 35-40 cookies

NOTES

_____

_____

_____

_____

_____

GUMBO FESTIVAL
Bridge City, Louisiana

Most Louisiana cities have a unique "claim to fame" and Bridge City is no exception. It is home to some of the best recipes of a Louisiana dish known 'round the world — Gumbo. As the "Gumbo Capital of the World," Bridge City has been celebrating its claim at an annual festival which began as a modest fundraiser for Holy Guardian Angels Church in the early 1970s.

Bridge City, appropriately named for its site at the base of Huey P. Long Bridge on the west bank of the Mississippi River across from New Orleans, turns into a grand food celebration during this festival in October which draws crowds from across the state. It even features its own 5K Run over the bridge on Sunday morning. Over 2,000 gallons of the famous gumbo, both seafood and chicken/sausage, is prepared for the visitors. While standing, sitting or walking, visitors are all seen enjoying the bayou delicacy from cups as they share in the excitement of the festival. Of course, many other native Louisiana foods such as jambalaya and red beans and rice, along with the traditional favorites, hamburgers and hotdogs, can also be found here.

Since a festival that celebrates food would not be complete without a little competition, the Gumbo Cooking Contest challenges the Cajun cooks to make their best creation of the dish. And the champion of this contest carries the title proudly, since he or she is chosen by a distinguished panel of celebrity chefs who meet in the church rectory to select the prized rendition. The judges represent many of the finest restaurants in and around New Orleans.

Continuous live entertainment from local bands playing Cajun, Country, Zydeco, Jazz, Blues and Rock music provide a focal point for the outdoor activities, while the fais-do-do area prompts many participants to get up and dance. As an added attraction, Miss Creole Gumbo and her king are usually on hand to greet the visitors.

Lagniappe

This festival is a great way to build a weekend getaway, and since it is literally conducted across the bridge from New Orleans, a visit would not be complete without a trip to the internationally-famous city. There activities abound and attractions are endless. Restaurants choices number in the hundreds from world-famous establishments such as Brennan's to small, casual bistros. Riverboat cruises along the Mississippi River and swamp tours through Louisiana's bayous are among visitors' favorites. Lodging options range from famed classic hotels such as the Royal Sonesta to a multitude of quaint bed-and-breakfast options such as the lovely 14-room Corn Stalk Hotel on Royal Street wrapped in its classic wrought-iron corn stalk fence. Exit at I-10 at Huey P. Long Bridge, travel south on Clearview Parkway, cross Huey P. Long Bridge and take an immediate right. You will travel straight to the festival grounds at Angel Square, 1701 Bridge City Avenue. Admission is free. Call (504) 436-4712.

Photo: José L. Garcia, II
A bowl of Chicken and Sausage Gumbo and the Peanut Ware Antique Cast Iron Pot.

CHICKEN & ANDOUILLE GUMBO

INGREDIENTS:

1 (4-5 pound) stewing hen, cut into serving pieces

1 pint oysters

1 pound andouille, cut into 1-inch slices

1 cup vegetable oil

1½ cups flour

2 cups chopped onions

2 cups chopped celery

1 cup chopped bell pepper

¼ cup diced garlic

3 quarts chicken stock

1 pint chicken livers

2 cups sliced green onions

¼ cup chopped parsley

salt and black pepper

Louisiana Gold Pepper Sauce

METHOD:

In a 2-gallon stock pot, heat oil over medium-high heat. Once oil is hot, add flour and, using a wire whisk, stir constantly until roux is golden brown. Do not scorch. Should black specks appear, discard and begin again. Add onions, celery, bell pepper and garlic. Saute 3-5 minutes or until vegetables are wilted. Add hen, blend into vegetable mixture and saute 15 minutes. Add chicken stock, one ladle at a time. Reduce heat to simmer and cook approximately 1 hour. Add chicken livers, andouille and oysters. Cook an additional 10 minutes. Blend in green onions and parsley and continue to simmer until chicken is tender and fully cooked. Season to taste using salt, pepper and Louisiana Gold. Serve over cooked rice.

PREP TIME: 1½ hours   SERVES: 6

NOTES

_____

_____

_____

_____

_____

_____

SHRIMP, CRAB & OKRA GUMBO

INGREDIENTS:

2 pounds (35 count) shrimp, peeled and deveined
1 pound jumbo lump crabmeat
2 pounds fresh okra
$\frac{1}{2}$ cup vegetable oil
1 cup chopped onions
1 cup chopped celery
$\frac{1}{2}$ cup chopped bell pepper
2 tbsps diced garlic
1 cup vegetable oil

1 cup flour
1 cup diced tomatoes
1 (8 ounce) can tomato sauce
3 quarts shellfish stock
1 cup sliced green onions
$\frac{1}{2}$ cup chopped parsley
salt and cracked pepper
Louisiana Gold Pepper Sauce

METHOD:

In a 12-inch cast iron skillet, heat $\frac{1}{2}$ cup of vegetable oil over medium-high heat. Add okra, onions, celery, bell pepper and garlic. Slowly saute the mixed vegetables until the okra is well cooked and slightly browned. You must stir this mixture constantly as the okra will tend to stick and scorch. Once it is cooked, remove from heat and set aside. In a 5-quart cast iron dutch oven, heat remaining vegetable oil over medium-high heat. Add flour and, using a wire whisk, whip until dark brown roux is achieved. Add tomatoes and tomato sauce and stir to incorporate well. Pour off the excess oil from the okra mixture and add the contents of the skillet to the roux. Blend well and slowly add the hot shellfish stock, one ladle at a time, until all is incorporated. Bring to a rolling boil and reduce to simmer. More stock may be needed to maintain a soup-like consistency. Add green onions and parsley. Season to taste using salt, pepper and Louisiana Gold. Cook for 15 minutes. Add shrimp and cook 10-15 minutes longer. Add lump crabmeat and adjust seasonings if necessary. Serve over steamed white rice. Garnish with a dash of Zatarain's file powder prior to serving.

PREP TIME: 1 hour   SERVES: 12

NOTES

_____

_____

_____

_____

_____

_____

MY SPECIAL POTATO SALAD

INGREDIENTS:

12 medium new potatoes

³/₄ cup chopped celery

¹/₂ cup chopped red bell pepper

¹/₄ cup chopped green olives

¹/₂ cup chopped sweet pickle relish

1 cup mayonnaise

¹/₂ cup sour cream

2 tbsps prepared mustard

2 tbsps sweet pickle juice

4 boiled egg yolks, diced

¹/₂ cup sliced green onions

2 tsps salt

1 tsp black pepper

METHOD:

Boil potatoes in salted water until tender. Drain under cold running water and allow to cool slightly. Dice potatoes into ¹/₂-inch cubes. In a large mixing bowl, place potatoes and all remaining ingredients. Mix well to incorporate all ingredients. Refrigerate prior to serving.

PREP TIME: 45 minutes   SERVES: 6

WHITE RICE

INGREDIENTS:

1 cup long grain rice

1¹/₂ cups water

1 tbsp butter

salt

METHOD:

Wash rice under cold water at least twice. Place in a 3-quart cast iron sauce pan with water, butter and salt. Bring to a rapid boil, uncovered. Reduce heat to simmer, cover and cook 30 minutes. DO NOT STIR OR REMOVE LID DURING COOKING PROCESS.

PREP TIME: 45 minutes   SERVES: 6

NOTES

_____

_____

_____

_____

_____

JALEPENO CORN BREAD

INGREDIENTS:

1 (4-ounce) can jalapeno peppers,
    drained and chopped
1$^{1}/_{2}$ cups yellow corn meal
1 tbsp sugar
1 tbsp baking powder
1 tsp salt

1 cup milk
2 large eggs
1 (8 $^{3}/_{4}$-ounce) can cream style corn
$^{1}/_{4}$ cup shortening
1$^{1}/_{2}$ cups sharp cheddar cheese, grated

METHOD:

Preheat oven to 425 degrees F. Grease a 8$^{1}/_{2}$" x 4$^{1}/_{2}$" x 2$^{1}/_{2}$" loaf pan. Sift all dry ingredients and set aside. In a medium bowl, place milk, eggs, corn and shortening. Using an electric mixer, combine until well blended. Add dry corn meal, sugar, baking powder and salt. Add cheese and peppers, stirring until totally incorporated. Pour batter into loaf pan and bake 35 minutes or until golden brown.

PREP TIME: 45 minutes   MAKES: 1 loaf

NOTES

_____

_____

_____

_____

_____

WASHINGTON PARISH FREE FAIR
Franklinton, Louisiana

For over 80 years, visitors have traveled to the far eastern corner of Louisiana to gather in Washington Parish for the largest county fair, by attendance, in the United States. The festivities of the Washington Parish Free Fair are conducted each October for four days, and many of the fair highlights are centered around historical Mile Branch Settlement, located on the Washington Parish Fairgrounds. This beautiful settlement began as a tribute to the pioneering spirit of Washington Parish residents. Visitors will undoubtedly leave the fair each year with an increased knowledge of the heritage, innovation and ingenuity of the pioneers from the early days of Washington Parish.

Throughout the settlement, you will find dedicated volunteers, many of whom are direct descendants of the early pioneers, who have extensive knowledge of the history of each cabin and structure. They graciously share their insight with the visitors.

As you walk the grounds, you will find an aroma of wood smoke coming from the fireplaces of authentic log cabins. You will see reenactments of country life and cooking — corn ground into fresh corn meal, syrup prepared in an open kettle, iron shaped at the blacksmith shop, sheep sheared in the barnyard, quilts sewn on the front porches of the cabins, and much more.

Don't miss the unique foods at this festival which include cracklins, Indian Fry Bread, which is rolled flat and deep fried, and sassafras tea, just to name a few. This great fair also features a parade, midway, rodeo and, of course, great musical concerts, including performances by choirs from local churches at the Half-Moon Bluff Baptist Church on the settlement.

The Washington Parish Free Fair is a great way to spend a few days of the beautiful fall month of October. Don't miss the chance to take in the sights and sounds of this historic area of Louisiana and sample country living from years past.

Lagniappe

Washington Parish is located at the far east end of Louisiana and borders Mississippi. The route to Franklinton is a scenic one through bayou country, with many small country towns to see along the way. You may want to stay at Sha-Tims bed-and-breakfast and try a meal at Main Street Cafe or the Riverside Restaurant. Neighboring parishes of Tangipahoa to the west and St. Tammany to the south also offer an abundance of sight-seeing, family entertainment and dining options.

Travel on I-55 to the Amite Exit at Highway 16. Travel East on Highway 16 to Highway 25 and turn left to Franklinton. For more information, contact the Washington Parish Fair Association at (504) 839-3403.

Photo: Jose´ L. Garcia, II
Clockwise from bottom left: Scripture Cake, Chicken and Wine Casserole.

CABBAGE PATCH SOUP

INGREDIENTS:

3 cups finely shredded cabbage

2 tbsps margarine

1 pound lean ground beef

1 medium onion, thinly sliced

1/2 cup diced celery

1/4 cup diced red bell pepper

1/4 cup diced garlic

1 (15-ounce) can tomatoes with juice

2 cups water

1 can red kidney beans

1 tsp chili powder

salt and black pepper

Louisiana Gold Pepper Sauce

METHOD:

In a 5-quart cast iron dutch oven, melt margarine over medium-high heat. Add ground beef and cook until meat is thoroughly cooked and separated, grain for grain. Add onions, celery, bell pepper and garlic. Saute 3-5 minutes or until vegetables are wilted. Add tomatoes and, using the back of a spoon, break tomatoes into the meat/vegetable mixture. Add water and beans, blending well until all is incorporated. Add cabbage, bring mixture to a rolling boil, reduce to simmer and cook until cabbage is tender. Season to taste using chili powder, salt, pepper and Louisiana Gold.

PREP TIME: 1 hour   SERVES: 6

NOTES

_____

_____

_____

_____

_____

_____

MILE BRANCH ONION SHORTCAKE

INGREDIENTS FOR CRUST:

2 cups sifted all purpose flour

4 tsps baking powder

1 tsp salt

6 tbsps butter

$^1/_2$ cup buttermilk

METHOD:

In a large mixing bowl, combine flour, baking powder and salt. Cut in butter with a pastry blender until mixture is crumbly. Gradually stir in buttermilk until well blended. Turn out onto a lightly floured surface. Knead until dough is smooth. Roll dough between 2 sheets of floured wax paper to a 15-inch round. Fit into a 9-inch ($1^1/_2$-inch high) springform pan, pressing firmly against the side. Trim top edge of pastry even with the top edge of the pan. Chill.

INGREDIENTS FOR FILLING:

8 medium onions, thinly sliced

6 tbsps butter

6 eggs

$^1/_2$ cup cream

1 pint sour cream

1 tsp salt

$^1/_4$ tsp pepper

$^1/_4$ cup chopped parsley

METHOD:

Preheat oven to 450 degrees F. In a 10-inch cast iron skillet, melt butter over medium-high heat. Add onions and saute until wilted, approximately 10-15 minutes. Allow onions to cool then spoon into prepared pie crust. In a mixing bowl, place eggs and beat slightly. Add cream and sour cream and blend well. Season to taste using salt and pepper. Pour egg/cream mixture over the onions and bake for 10 minutes. Reduce temperature to 350 degrees F and bake for an additional 45 minutes. Garnish with parsley prior to serving.

PREP TIME: $1^1/_2$ hours   SERVES: 8

NOTES

_____

_____

_____

_____

_____

_____

SCRIPTURE CAKE

INGREDIENTS:

1 cup butter, softened (Judges 5:25)

2 cups sugar (Jeremiah 6:20)

1 tbsp honey (Exodus 16:31)

6 eggs (Isaiah 10:14)

3 cups all purpose flour (Kings 4:22)

2 tsps baking powder (Corinthians 5:6)

½ tsp salt (Leviticus 2:13)

1 tsp cinnamon (Kings 10:10)

¼ tsp cloves (Kings 10:10)

¼ tsp ginger (Kings 10:10)

½ cup all purpose flour (Kings 4:22)

1 cup water (Exodus 17:6)

2 cups raisins (Samuel 30:12)

2 cups figs (Samuel 30:12)

1 cup chopped almonds (Genesis 43:11)

METHOD:

Preheat oven to 325 degrees F. In a large mixing bowl cream butter and sugar. Add honey and blend well. Add eggs, one at a time, beating after each addition. In another mixing bowl, combine 3 cups of flour, baking powder, salt and spices. Add to creamed mixture alternately with water. Beat well. Dredge raisins, figs and almonds in remaining ½ cup of flour. Gently stir fruits and nuts into batter. Grease and flour 2 loaf pans. Spoon batter into pans and bake for 1 hour and 15 minutes.

PREP TIME: 1 hour and 45 minutes   MAKES: 2 loaves

NOTES

_____

_____

_____

_____

_____

_____

CHICKEN & WINE CASSEROLE

INGREDIENTS:

1 whole fryer

$^1/_4$ cup vegetable oil

12 small onions

1 bay leaf

1 tbsp chopped onions

1 cup whole mushrooms

4 cloves of garlic, crushed

2 cups chicken broth

1 cup red wine

$^1/_2$ tsp dried thyme

$^1/_2$ tsp dried basil

salt and black pepper

METHOD:

Preheat oven to 325 degrees F. Cut chicken into 8 serving pieces. In a 10-inch cast iron skillet, heat oil over medium-high heat. Brown chicken well on all sides until golden brown. Remove and drain. Add onions, bay leaf, chopped onions, mushrooms and garlic. Pour in chicken broth and red wine. Season to taste using thyme, basil, salt and pepper. Return chicken to pan and bake, covered, for 1$^1/_2$ hours or until tender. Serve over pasta or rice.

PREP TIME: 2 hours   SERVES: 6

MISS STELLA MAGEE'S RAISIN PIE

INGREDIENTS:

1$^1/_2$ cups sugar

3 eggs

1 tbsp butter

2 tbsps flour

2 tbsps water

2 tbsps vinegar

$^2/_3$ cup raisins

$^2/_3$ cup pecan pieces

1 tsp cinnamon

9-inch pie shell

METHOD:

Preheat oven to 350 degrees F. In a large mixing bowl, combine all ingredients until well blended. Pour into unbaked pie shell and bake 30-45 minutes. Serve warm.

PREP TIME: 1 hour   SERVES: 8

NOTES

_____

_____

_____

_____

_____

_____

YAMBILEE FESTIVAL
Opelousas, Louisiana

It is no coincidence that one of the oldest festivals in Louisiana is conducted each year in one of the state's oldest settlements. Opelousas has been the site of the Yambilee Festival during the last full week in October since 1946. The third oldest settlement in Louisiana, founded in 1720, Opelousas was settled by the French who discovered the Native Americans eating the delicacy for which this popular festival is named — the yam, or sweet potato to many of us.

The idea for the Yambilee was conceived by J.W. "Bill" Low, a native Texan who adopted the City of Opelousas as his home, and his friend Felix Dezauche, a yam shipper and processor, as they enjoyed a cup of coffee together. Ever since that first festival, a Yambilee Queen has been crowned, thus making this tradition one of the festival highlights. Her king is announced in grand style two Saturdays before the festival.

The organizers of this festival take their contests very seriously. Festival-goers participate in one of the widest array of categories of any Louisiana festival. These popular contests are highlighted by the National Sweet Potato Show with divisions featuring the sweet potato fresh, canned and cooked — just to mention a few. One of the most popular divisions each year, however, takes the most unique twist by showcasing Yam-I-Mals, or Sweet Potatoes which have been harvested with striking features that resemble animals. Of course, the Yam-I-Mals are on display in the festival's Yamatorium.

Other festival highlights include the Yam Auction, the Grand Louisyam Parade, an Arts and Crafts Show, a Garden Show and plenty of live music on the Yambilee Grounds.

Lagniappe

While visiting Opelousas, do not miss dining at the Palace Cafe, a landmark on Main Street for over 70 years. Be sure to tour the turn-of-the-century home Yesterday and Le Vieux Village du Poste d'Opelousas on Highway 190. The neighboring town of Washington, only 10 miles away, offers bed-and-breakfast lodging and is a fabulous antique town. And remember, a drive to the Acadiana city of Lafayette is a mere 20 miles to the south. While driving through Carencro to get to Opelousas, look up Murray Conque, a Cajun humorist that performs in local establishments.

Travel on I-49 to Opelousas, Exit Highway 190 West, travel 3 miles to the festival grounds. For more information, write to Louisiana Yambilee, Inc., P.O. Box 444, Opelousas, LA 70570 or call (800) 210-5298 or (318) 948-8848.

Photo: José L. Garcia, II
Clockwise from bottom left: A bowl of Candied Yam and White Chocolate Ice Cream.

CANDIED YAM FLAN

INGREDIENTS:

1 cup Bruce's candied yams, reserve syrup
1 1/2 cups milk
1 cup heavy whipping cream
4 whole eggs
4 egg yolks

1/2 cup sugar
1/4 tsp cinnamon
1/4 tsp nutmeg
1 tbsp vanilla
1 tbsp praline liqueur

METHOD:

Preheat oven to 350 degrees F. In the bowl of a food processor, combine yams in syrup, milk, whipping cream, eggs and egg yolks. Blend until yams are pureed and mixture is well blended. Pour ingredients into a mixing bowl and add sugar, cinnamon, nutmeg, vanilla and praline liqueur. Using a wire whisk, blend gently until sugar is dissolved and spices are incorporated. Pour the mixture into 8 custard ramekins or 1 large flan mold. Place the cups or mold into a baking pan with 1-inch lip. Place pan on the center shelf of the oven. Pour about 1/2-inch of water into the baking pan to act as a water bath. Bake 45 minutes to 1 hour for the cups or 1 1/2 hours for the mold. Insert a tester into the custard to ensure that it has set properly prior to removing from the oven. The custard is best when chilled overnight.

PREP TIME: 2 Hours   SERVES: 8

NOTES

_____

_____

_____

_____

_____

_____

MOIST & YUMMY YAM CAKE

INGREDIENTS:

2 cups sugar

1 ½ cups vegetable oil

4 eggs

2 cups all purpose flour

3 tsps baking powder

3 tsps baking soda

1 tsp salt

2 tsps cinnamon

1 tbsp vanilla

1 cup chopped pecans

1 ½ cups Bruce's mashed yams

1 (20-ounce) can crushed pineapple

1 cup sugar

2 ½ tbsps corn starch

8 ounces cream cheese

½ stick butter

1 pound powdered sugar

1 tbsp vanilla

METHOD:

Preheat oven to 350 degrees F. Oil and flour three 9-inch cake pans. Set aside. In a large mixing bowl, cream sugar and oil until well blended. Add eggs, one at a time, whipping after each addition. In a separate bowl, combine flour, baking powder, soda, salt and cinnamon. Add dry mixture, a little at a time, into the egg mixture, blending well until all is incorporated. Fold in the vanilla, pecans and mashed yams. Once all is well blended, pour evenly into the cake pans. Bake 40 minutes or until cake tester comes out clean. While cake is baking, make filling by combining pineapple, sugar and corn starch in a 3-quart cast iron dutch oven. Bring to a low boil over medium-high heat, stirring constantly for 5 minutes. Once mixture thickens, remove from heat and allow filling to cool. In the bowl of an electric mixer, combine cream cheese, butter, powdered sugar and vanilla. Blend on low speed until well mixed. Whip until icing is fluffy and smooth. Remove and set aside. When cakes are done, remove from oven and allow to cool. Remove from baking pans and spread pineapple filling between layers. Ice with the cream cheese frosting and serve.

PREP TIME: 1 Hour   SERVES: 8-10

NOTES

_____

_____

_____

_____

_____

_____

CANDIED YAM & WHITE CHOCOLATE ICE CREAM

INGREDIENTS:

1 (16-ounce) can Bruce's candied yams
12 ounces white chocolate
1 $\frac{1}{2}$ cups sugar
1 $\frac{1}{2}$ cups water
8 egg yolks

$\frac{1}{2}$ tsp nutmeg
$\frac{1}{2}$ tsp cinnamon
1 tbsp vanilla
3 cups heavy whipping cream

METHOD:

Mash yams with syrup until fine puree is achieved. Chill in refrigerator for later use. Place the white chocolate in a stainless steel bowl over a pot of 120 degree F water until chocolate is totally melted. Stir occasionally to maintain a liquid state. In a 1-quart sauce pan, combine sugar and water. Stir well and bring to a low boil. Using a candy thermometer, bring the simple syrup to 234 degrees F, which is the soft-ball state. While syrup is heating, place egg yolks in the bowl of an electric mixer. Blend on low speed until eggs are slightly whipped. Once syrup has reached 234 degrees F, slowly pour the mixture into the eggs, whipping on medium speed. Take special care as the sugar will be extremely hot. Continue to whip eggs on medium-high until thick, approximately 5 minutes. Pour in the melted white chocolate and add the nutmeg, cinnamon and vanilla. Continue to blend until all is incorporated. Reduce speed to low and pour in whipping cream. Remove beaters and, using a rubber spatula, fold in the pureed candied yams. Place the entire mixture in the refrigerator until well chilled, preferably overnight. Freeze mixture in a home-style ice cream freezer according to manufacturer's directions

PREP TIME: 1 hour   MAKES: 2 quarts

NOTES

_____

_____

_____

_____

_____

_____

YAM-STUFFED SUGAR CURED HAM

INGREDIENTS:

1 (6-7 pound) boneless sugar-cured ham
¹/₄ cup butter
1 (20-ounce) can Bruce's cut yams
6 Bartlett or Bosc pears
2 cups Burgundy wine
2 cups sugar
1 quart water
¹/₂ cup chopped onions
¹/₂ cup chopped celery
¹/₄ cup chopped red bell pepper

¹/₂ cup chopped green bell pepper
¹/₄ cup diced garlic
¹/₄ cup raisins
¹/₄ cup fig preserves
¹/₂ cup chopped pecans
pinch of cinnamon
pinch of nutmeg
pinch of file´(optional)
salt and black pepper
2 (1.5-ounce) packages Bruce's original yam glaze

METHOD:

Preheat oven to 350 degrees F. Peel pears, leaving the stem in place. In a 1-gallon sauce pot, combine wine, sugar, water and pears. Poach for approximately 45 minutes or until pears are fork tender but not mushy. Remove and cool. When pears are cool, split them in half from top to bottom. Reserve 8 halves for decoration and dice the remaining 4 halves into 1/4-inch cubes. Drain the yams, reserving the liquid, and dice yams into 1/4-inch cubes. In a 10-inch cast iron skillet, melt butter over medium -high heat. Add onions, celery, bell pepper and garlic. Saute until vegetables are wilted, approximately 3-5 minutes. Add pears, raisins and figs. Continue to saute until mixture is well blended and resembles a chutney or stuffing. Season with a pinch of cinnamon, nutmeg and file. Fold in yams and pecans, remove from heat and cool. This may be done one day ahead. Slice ham horizontally across the middle and spread the center of ham with stuffing mixture about 3/4-inch thick. Top with the upper section of the ham, creating a sandwich effect. Place stuffed ham in a large roasting pan with lid. Garnish top of ham with pear halves in a decorative manner and secure the pears and the top of the ham with 6-inch wooden skewers. Prepare the yam glaze sauce according to package directions. If a thinner sauce is desired, you may add a touch of water or pineapple juice. Pour the glaze over the top of the ham prior to baking. You may wish to get more creative by adding orange slices, cherries and mint leaves in the decorations. Pour the yam juice into the baking pan and bake, covered, for 1 hour or until ham is heated thoroughly. Remove cover and allow ham to brown slightly.

PREP TIME: 1 1/2 Hours   SERVES: 6-8   NOTES

_____

_____

_____

_____

_____

BAYOU TECHE PORK & YAM BREAKFAST SAUSAGE

INGREDIENTS:

5 pounds ground pork
1 (16 ounce) can Bruce's yams, drained
1 tbsp black pepper
1 ½ tbsps rubbed sage
1 tsp ginger
1 ½ tsps nutmeg

2 tsps dried thyme
1 tbsp cayenne pepper
2 tbsps salt
1 ½ tbsps granulated garlic
¼ cup chopped parsley
1 cup iced water

METHOD:

When making sausage of any type, it is always best to keep the meat chilled to 35-40 degrees F. The iced water in the recipe maintains the cold temperature in the meat and sets the fat in the sausage. Slice the drained yams and dice into 1/4-inch cubes. Place the cubes on a cookie sheet and freeze for later use. In a large mixing bowl, combine all of the above ingredients except yams. Using your hands, mix the sausage well, turning and pushing the meat 10-15 minutes to ensure proper blending. Gently fold in the frozen yams. NOTE: Freezing the yams will guarantee a solid 1/4-inch cube which will be visible in the finished sausage. Roll the sausage into 3-inch patties or stuff into hog casing and tie off 6-inch links. Cook in the same method as any other breakfast sausage or grill the links over charcoal.

PREP TIME: 1 hour   MAKES: 25-30 (3-ounce) patties

NOTES

_____
_____
_____
_____
_____
_____

Chapter Nine
November

Los Islenos Festival
Louisiana Pecan Festival

LOS ISLENOS FESTIVAL
St. Bernard, Louisiana

They were Canary Islanders who settled in Louisiana between 1778 and 1783, coming to help Spain defend New Orleans against British invasion. They were settled in four locations, strategically placed around New Orleans to guard approaches to the city. They are called Islenos. It is as a tribute to these islanders, the people and the culture, that the Los Islenos Festival is conducted each March in St. Bernard Parish, just south of New Orleans.

Modern communications and transportation are making the Islenos less dependent on their traditional lifestyles. However, when you travel through the Islenos communities you can sense the community spirit of hard work and sharing that has endured for more than 200 years. This cultural festival honoring the early Islenos people is held in the village of St. Bernard just south of Chalmette. An Islenos Center, a unit of the Jean Lafitte Historical Park and Preserve, illustrates the culture of the people through arts and crafts and photo displays which depict the Isleno way of life.

During the two-day festival, visitors can enjoy Canary Island dancers, music by Spanish artists, boat building and other historical demonstrations, and plenty of great authentic foods of the culture.

Try the Caldo, one of their most famous dishes. This soup is made with beans, corn and potatoes and finished with cabbage and smoked meats. You can also try the cornmeal-fried oysters or a steaming bowl of gumbo.

Today, thousands of Isleno descendants live throughout the metropolitan New Orleans area. Nevertheless, the elderly Islenos still speak a Spanish dialect brought to Louisiana more than two centuries ago. They have preserved, to a large extent, their distinct cultural identity. Today, the Isleno communities of eastern St. Bernard Parish survive as the last living vestige of Spanish Colonial Louisiana.

Lagniappe

St. Bernard Parish is located just south of New Orleans and fronts the Gulf of Mexico. While in St. Bernard Parish, you will want to visit the Chalmette National Historic Park which preserves the site of the Battle of New Orleans, the greatest American land victory of the War of 1812. Also interesting and pertinent to the lives of the Islenos people are the Magnolia Plantation and the St. Bernard Cemetery, one of the oldest burial grounds in Louisiana. For dining, try Jr's Restaurant, owned by Isleno Henry "Junior" Rodriguez, specializing in boiled and fried seafood. Jean Lafitte Restaurant and Rocky & Carlo's are also good choices. Travel on I-10 to I-510/Chalmette. Travel on I-510 to Highway 39 East, stay on Highway 39 about 8 miles. For more information about the festival, call the Los Islenos Heritage & Cultural Society at (504) 682-2713.

Photo: Jose´ L. Garcia, II
Clockwise from bottom left: Islenos Paella, Mirliton Pie.

ISLENOS PAELLA

INGREDIENTS:

2 pounds Cajun venison sausage, sliced
1 pound chaurice, sliced
$\frac{1}{2}$ cup vegetable oil
2 cups chopped onions
1 cup chopped celery
$\frac{1}{2}$ cup chopped red bell pepper
$\frac{1}{4}$ cup diced garlic
1 (15-ounce) can tomato sauce

1 pound crawfish tails
5 cups water
$\frac{1}{2}$ cup sliced green onions
$\frac{1}{2}$ cup chopped parsley
3 cups Uncle Ben's converted rice
salt and black pepper
Louisiana Gold Pepper Sauce

METHOD:

In a 7-quart cast iron dutch oven, heat oil over medium high heat. Add venison sausage and chaurice. Cook until meat is golden brown and fat is rendered, approximately 10 minutes. Add onions, celery, bell pepper and garlic. Saute 3-5 minutes or until vegetables are wilted. Add tomato sauce and crawfish tails. Cook until sauce has come to a low simmer. Stir occasionally and simmer an additional 10 minutes. Add water and bring mixture to a rolling boil. Reduce heat to simmer and season to taste using salt, pepper and Louisiana Gold. Fold in rice, blending well into the seasoned liquid. Cover, reduce heat to low and cook 20 minutes. Top with green onions and parsley. Cover and cook an additional 10-15 minutes. Remove from heat and allow paella to steam, covered, 20 minutes prior to serving.

PREP TIME: 1 hour   SERVES: 6-8

NOTES

_____

_____

_____

_____

_____

MIRLITON PIE

INGREDIENTS:

2 cups cooked mirlitons, mashed

1 cup sugar

3 eggs, well beaten

1 cup biscuit mix

$\frac{1}{2}$ cup milk

$\frac{1}{4}$ cup melted butter

1 tbsp vanilla

$\frac{1}{8}$ tsp nutmeg

$\frac{1}{8}$ tsp cinnamon

9-inch unbaked pie shell

METHOD:

Preheat oven to 350 degrees F. Slice approximately 6-8 mirlitons lengthwise and remove the seed from the center of each. Place the mirliton in a large pot and cover by 2 inches with lightly salted cold water. Bring to a rolling boil and cook until mirliton is extremely tender. Drain and cool. Using a tablespoon, scoop the tender meat from the outer shell, draining it in a colander and discarding the shell. Once mirliton is well drained, measure 2 full cups. In a large mixing bowl, combine sugar and eggs. Using a wire whisk, blend well. Sprinkle in biscuit mix, alternately with the milk and melted butter. When well blended, add vanilla, nutmeg and cinnamon. Fold in the mashed mirliton. Pour mixture into a prepared pie shell and bake for 45-50 minutes or until done. This dish is in many ways similar to bread pudding and can be eaten either as a dessert or vegetable.

PREP TIME: 1 hour   SERVES: 8

NOTES

_____

_____

_____

_____

_____

_____

BOILED PUDDING

INGREDIENTS:

2 cups plain yellow cake mix

4 cups self-rising flour

1 cup sugar

3 eggs, beaten

½ cup oil

⅔ cup water

1 cup golden raisins

1 cup black raisins

2 tsps vanilla

1 tsp cinnamon

1 tsp nutmeg

2 cups cream anglaise

METHOD:

Fill a 12-quart stock pot with cold water, allowing 2 inches of space to the top. Bring water to a rolling boil and reduce to a low simmer, adding water as necessary to retain volume. In a large mixing bowl combine cake mix, flour and sugar. Add eggs, oil, water and raisins. Blend mixture well to combine all ingredients. Flavor the dough with vanilla, cinnamon and nutmeg. Form the dough into a ball and powder lightly with flour. Place the ball into the center of a cheese cloth that measures approximately 3 feet square and is doubled. Pull all the edges of the cheese cloth above the dough and tie tightly to close all ends, leaving approximately 4 inches from the dough to the tie to allow for expansion. This 4-inch space is extremely important as the dough will rise substantially during the cooking. Place the cheese cloth into the simmering water, weighing the pudding down with a platter or bowl to keep it submerged. Simmer the pudding 1½-2 hours or until a cake tester comes out clean. Remove from simmering water and allow to cool, approximately 1 hour. Cut the pudding in quarters and place in a large mixing bowl or platter. Top with the cream anglaise (see recipe) and place in the refrigerator to absorb the sauce. Serve as you would any cold dessert.

PREP TIME: 3 hours   SERVES: 6-8

NOTES

_____

_____

_____

_____

_____

_____

Praline Cream Anglaise

INGREDIENTS:

3 cups heavy whipping cream
1 cup sugar
pinch of cinnamon
pinch of nutmeg

1 tbsp vanilla
4 egg yolks, beaten
1 tbsp corn starch
$\frac{1}{4}$ cup praline or hazelnut liqueur

METHOD:

In a 3-quart cast iron sauce pan, scald whipping cream over medium-high heat. In a separate mixing bowl, combine sugar, cinnamon, nutmeg, vanilla, eggs and corn starch. Using a wire whip, blend until well mixed and creamy. Add liqueur and fold once or twice until blended. Into the mixing bowl, ladle one cup of hot cream, stirring constantly while pouring. Transfer egg mixture to the pot of hot cream, whisking constantly with a wire whip. Cook one or two minutes and remove from heat. Should mixture become too thick, add a little cold whipping cream.

YIELDS: 3 cups

NOTES

_____

_____

_____

_____

_____

CALDO

INGREDIENTS:

1 pound white beans
1 pound diced ham
1 pound pickled meat
$^1/_2$ cup vegetable oil
2 cups diced onions
1 cup diced celery
1 cup diced bell pepper
$^1/_4$ cup diced garlic
2 (8-ounce) cans tomato sauce
1 gallon cold water
1 (15-ounce) can string beans

1 (15-ounce) can mustard greens
1 (15-ounce) can spinach
1 (15-ounce) can corn
1 (15-ounce) can peas
1 (15-ounce) can sweet potatoes
1 (15-ounce) can squash
1 (15-ounce) can Irish potatoes
1$^1/_2$ heads shredded cabbage
2 ears corn, sliced
salt and black pepper
Louisiana Gold Pepper Sauce

METHOD:

In a 12-quart cast iron dutch oven, heat oil over medium-high heat. Add ham and pickled meat and saute until golden brown. Add onions, celery, bell pepper and garlic. Saute 3-5 minutes or until vegetables are wilted. Add white beans, tomato sauce and water. Bring mixture to a rolling boil and continue to cook until beans are tender, approximately 1 hour. Add all canned vegetables, along with cabbage and fresh corn. Continue to cook on medium heat for approximately 30 minutes. Season to taste using salt, pepper and Louisiana Gold. You may need to add water as mixture cooks in order to retain volume. Serve as a soup over steamed white rice.

PREP TIME: 2 hours   SERVES: 8

NOTES

_____

_____

_____

_____

_____

Smoked Duck, Oyster & Andouille Gumbo

INGREDIENTS:

2 Long Island ducks, smoked and cut
    into serving pieces
1 pint oysters
1 pound sliced andouille
1 cup vegetable oil
1¼ cups flour
2 cups chopped onions
2 cups chopped celery

1 cup chopped bell pepper
¼ cup diced garlic
3 quarts chicken stock
1 pint oyster liquor
2 cups sliced green onions
1 cup chopped parsley
salt and cracked pepper
Louisiana Gold Pepper Sauce

METHOD:

In a 2-gallon stock pot, heat oil over medium-high heat. Once oil is hot, add flour and, using a wire whisk, stir constantly until roux is golden brown. Do not scorch. Should black specks appear, discard and begin again. Add onions, celery, bell pepper and garlic. Saute 3-5 minutes or until vegetables are wilted. Add duck and andouille, blending into vegetable mixture. Add chicken stock and oyster liquor, one ladle at a time. Bring to a rolling boil, reduce to simmer and cook approximately 2 hours. When duck is tender, add oysters and cook an additional 10 minutes. Add green onions and parsley. Season to taste using salt, pepper and Louisiana Gold. Serve over steamed white rice.

PREP TIME: 2¹/₂₂ hours   SERVES: 6

NOTES

_____

_____

_____

_____

_____

_____

LOUISIANA PECAN FESTIVAL
Colfax, Louisiana

During the first weekend each November since 1969, Louisianians and visitors from around the country have gathered in central Louisiana in the small town of Colfax to celebrate the Louisiana Pecan Festival. One of the state's veteran festivals, the Pecan Festival began as part of the centennial anniversary celebration of Grant Parish to promote the ever-growing pecan industry.

Today, an estimated 100,000 people enjoy the two days of festivities which often spurs reunions of families and friends. Participants gather at the flag pole on Front Street on the first day of the festival for the traditional opening, the blessing of the crops. Locals believe this blessing aids in a prosperous and bountiful harvest year.

The railroad depot is converted into a country store and serves as a festival concession where the shelves are stocked with home-ground corn meal, ribbon cane syrup, jellies, and a wide array of crafts such as quilts, aprons, and bonnets — all handmade by the locals. Over 100 crafters from neighboring states display and sell their work as well.

The first day of the festival is declared "Children's Day." It is even a school holiday for the children in Grant Parish, so no child at this festival is seen complaining about enjoying games, contests and carnival rides instead of doing schoolwork.

On Saturday, crowds will line Front Street to catch a glimpse of the grand parade of bands, floats, dancers and beauty queens as they travel downtown. Keep your eye out for the Louisiana Pecan Festival Queen who is the center of attention at this event.

As you walk the grounds of the festival, you cannot miss the aroma of frontier sausage sandwiches, meat pies that festival staple, gumbo. Of course, the festival's namesake, the Louisiana Pecan, is also prepared in a variety of dishes. You will want a copy of the official festival publication, The Pecan Cookbook, to take home.

Other activities throughout this fun-filled weekend include a cooking contest, costume contest, log cutting contest, turkey shoot, trail ride and lots of carnival rides. A street dance and spectacular fireworks display will close out the festival on Saturday night.

So, listen to festival organizers when they say, "There is Something for Everyone at the Louisiana Pecan Festival."

Lagniappe

Colfax, Louisiana is located in central Louisiana on U.S. Highway 71 off of I-49. While visiting central Louisiana, try a stay at one of the Cotton Road Plantations which have bed-and-breakfast accommodations. Good choices are Loyd Hall Plantation, a beautiful 640-acre working cotton plantation and Magnolia Plantation, circa 1830s, which is beautifully furnished and has remained in the same family since the original French land grant of 1753.

Only 15 miles to the south, in Alexandria and Pineville, you will find all of the comforts of Southern hospitality. There you can try a meal at Cajun Landing Restaurant which offers a Cajun cottage setting and spend the night in one of the oldest hotels in the South, The Bentley.

About 45 miles north on I-49 is the oldest settlement in the Louisiana purchase, the scenic town of Natchitoches, established in 1714. It is not only the setting of the popular movie "Steel Magnolias," but is home to such famous plantations as Melrose and Magnolia.

Travel on I-49 to Alexandria, travel northwest on Highway 71 to downtown Colfax. For more information about the festival, call the Alexandria/Pineville Area Convention & Visitors Bureau at (800) 742-7049 or (318) 443-7049.

Photo: José L. Garcia, II
Super Moist Carrot Cake with Pralines

MEAT LOAF WITH PECAN STUFFING

INGREDIENTS:

3 pounds ground beef
$1/2$ cup chopped pecans
1 cup chopped onions
$1/2$ cup chopped celery
$1/4$ cup chopped red bell pepper
$1/4$ cup chopped yellow bell pepper
$1/4$ cup diced garlic
1 cup seasoned Italian bread crumbs

$1/2$ cup milk
2 eggs
$1/3$ cup shortening
2 cups whole wheat bread, diced
$3/4$ cup beef stock
1 tbsp Worcestershire sauce
salt and black pepper

METHOD:

Preheat oven to 350 degrees F. In a large mixing bowl, combine beef, onions, celery, bell peppers, garlic, bread crumbs, milk and one egg. Using your hands, mix all ingredients until well blended. Place $1/2$ of the mixture in the bottom of a greased loaf pan. Set aside. In a separate mixing bowl, combine remaining egg, shortening, whole wheat bread and beef stock. Mix thoroughly until all ingredients are well blended. Season to taste using Worcestershire, salt and pepper. Add chopped pecans and mix thoroughly. Spread the pecan stuffing on top of meat mixture and top with remaining meat mixture. Bake for $1\frac{1}{2}$ hours or until golden brown. Cool slightly prior to removing from pan. Slice and serve warm.

PREP TIME: 2 hours   SERVES: 10

NOTES

_____

_____

_____

_____

_____

_____

TROUT PRALINE

INGREDIENTS:

6 (5-8-ounce) trout fillets
¾ cup vegetable oil
eggwash (1 egg, ½ cup water, ½ cup milk, blended)
1 cup pecan flour
½ cup flour
1 tbsp diced garlic
½ cup sliced green onions

¾ cup chopped pecans
1½ ounces Frangelico liqueur
2 cups heavy whipping cream
4 pats cold butter
¼ cup chopped parsley
salt and black pepper
Louisiana Gold Pepper Sauce

METHOD:

You may purchase pecan flour from any specialty bake shop. Combine pecan flour and flour in a small mixing bowl. Season to taste using salt and pepper. In a 10-inch cast iron skillet, heat oil over medium-high heat. Dip fillets in eggwash and coat generously with flour. Saute fillets in hot oil until golden brown, 3-5 minutes on each side. Once done, remove from skillet and keep warm. In the same skillet, place garlic, green onions and pecans. Saute 3-5 minutes or until vegetables are wilted. Deglaze with Frangelico and add heavy whipping cream. Bring to a low boil and simmer until cream is reduced by ½ volume. Add cold butter, two pats at a time, swirling pan constantly until all is incorporated. Butter will finish sauce to a nice sheen. Add parsley and season to taste using salt, pepper and Louisiana Gold. Place sauce in the center of a serving plate and top with trout fillet.

PREP TIME: 1 hour   SERVES: 6

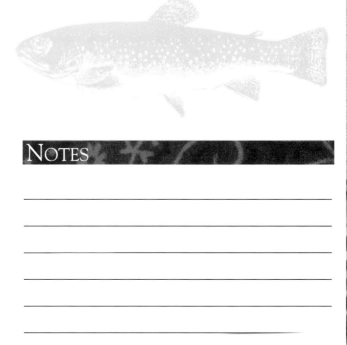

NOTES

_____

_____

_____

_____

_____

_____

PECAN HAM ROLL-UPS

INGREDIENTS:

10 slices smoked or boiled ham, cut 1/8-inch thick

1 cup mashed sweet potatoes

3 tbsps vegetable oil

$^{1}/_{2}$ cup crushed pineapple

$^{1}/_{2}$ cup seasoned Italian bread crumbs

3 tbsps sugar

$^{1}/_{4}$ cup chopped pecans

$^{3}/_{4}$ cup pineapple juice

salt and black pepper

METHOD:

Preheat oven to 350 degrees F. In a large mixing bowl, combine sweet potatoes, oil, pineapple, bread crumbs and sugar. Add pecans and mix all ingredients well. Spread this filling on the slices of ham and roll in jelly-roll fashion. Fasten each ham slice with toothpicks. Place in a 9" x 13" baking dish and cover with pineapple juice. Bake for 30 minutes, basting occasionally.

PREP TIME: $1^{1}/_{2}$ hours   SERVES: 3

CHUNKY CHICKEN SALAD, PLANTATION-STYLE

INGREDIENTS:

3 fried chicken breasts, skin on

$^{3}/_{4}$ cup mayonnaise

$^{1}/_{4}$ cup orange juice

$^{1}/_{4}$ cup heavy whipping cream

$^{1}/_{2}$ cup seedless green grapes, sliced

$^{1}/_{2}$ cup mandarin sections

$^{1}/_{2}$ cup toasted pecans, chopped

$^{1}/_{2}$ cup finely diced celery

$^{1}/_{4}$ cup chopped parsley

1 tbsp fresh thyme, chopped

1 tbsp fresh basil, chopped

salt and cracked pepper

Louisiana Gold Pepper Sauce

METHOD:

Remove meat from the breast bone, keeping skin intact, and cut into $^{3}/_{4}$-inch cubes. This is very important, since the seasoning on the fried chicken adheres to the skin and will help season the salad. Set aside. In a large mixing bowl, combine mayonnaise, orange juice and heavy whipping cream. Using a wire whisk, whip until the dressing is well blended. Season to taste using salt, pepper and Louisiana Gold. Add all remaining ingredients except chicken, blending well into dressing. Add cubed chicken and gently fold into the mixture. Once chicken is coated, adjust seasonings if necessary. Serve on fresh spinach or romaine lettuce leaves.

PREP TIME: 30 minutes   SERVES: 6

NOTES

_____

_____

_____

SUPER MOIST CARROT CAKE

INGREDIENTS:

3 cups grated carrots

2 cups sugar

1½ cups vegetable oil

4 eggs

2 cups all purpose flour

3 tsps baking powder

3 tsps baking soda

1 tsp salt

2 tsps cinnamon

1 tbsp vanilla

1 cup chopped pecans

1 (20-ounce) can crushed pineapple

1 cup sugar

2½ tbsps corn starch

8 ounces cream cheese

½ stick butter

1 pound powdered sugar

METHOD:

Preheat oven to 350 degrees F. Oil and flour four 9-inch cake pans. Set aside. In a large mixing bowl, cream sugar and oil until well blended. Add eggs, one at a time, whipping after each addition. In a separate bowl, combine flour, baking powder, soda, salt and cinnamon. Add, a little at a time, into the egg mixture, blending well until all is incorporated. Fold in ½ tablespoon of the vanilla, pecans and grated carrots. Once all is well blended, pour evenly into the four cake pans. Bake 30-40 minutes or until cake tester comes out clean. While cake is baking, make filling by combining pineapple, sugar and corn starch. Bring to a low boil over medium-high heat, stirring constantly for 5 minutes. Once mixture thickens, remove filling from heat and allow it to cool. In the bowl of an electric mixer, combine cream cheese, butter, powdered sugar and the remaining vanilla. Blend on low speed until well mixed. Increase speed and whip until icing is fluffy and smooth. Remove and set aside. When cakes are done, remove from oven and allow to cool. Remove from baking pans and spread pineapple filling between layers. Ice with the cream cheese frosting and serve.

PREP TIME: 1 hour   SERVES: 8-10

NOTES

_____

_____

_____

_____

_____

_____

Welcome to Louisiana!
Please sample our fairs and festivals!

Louisiana Specialty Products

When cooking the cuisine of South Louisiana, numerous specialty products such as cast iron pots, a 200-year old tradition, crawfish tails and andouille sausage are utilized. Most of these unique items are grown or manufactured here in our state.

At Chef John Folse & Company, we are able to make these unique items available to you anywhere in the country. If you are interested in purchasing or obtaining information on any of the products featured in this cookbook or on my PBS series, "A Taste of Louisiana with Chef John Folse & Company," please write or phone me at:

Chef John Folse & Company
2517 South Phillipe Avenue
Gonzales, LA 70737

(504) 644-6000
(504) 644-1295 Fax

Please visit us on the internet and take a walk through our Company Store at:

http://www.jfolse.com

We look forward to assisting you with any special product needs or additional information on the cuisine and culture of the Cajuns and Creoles!

NOTES

INDEX

APPETIZERS

SOUPS

SALADS

VEGETABLES

GAME

DESSERTS

LAGNIAPPE

BREADS